THE MARKETING REVOLUTION IN POLITICS

The Marketing
Revolution in Politics

*What Recent U.S. Presidential Campaigns
Can Teach Us about Effective Marketing*

BRUCE I. NEWMAN

UNIVERSITY OF TORONTO PRESS
Toronto Buffalo London

ISBN 978-1-4426-4799-2

Printed on acid-free, 100% post-consumer recycled paper with
vegetable-based inks.

Library and Archives Canada Cataloguing in Publication

Newman, Bruce I., author
The marketing revolution in politics : what recent U.S. presidential campaigns
can teach us about effective marketing / Bruce I. Newman.

Includes bibliographical references and index.
ISBN 978-1-4426-4799-2 (bound)

1. Political campaigns – United States.   2. Campaign management – United
States.   3. Advertising, Political – United States.   4. Communication in
politics – United States.   5. Marketing – Political aspects – United States.
I. Title.

JK2281.N49 2015   324.70973   C2015-905299-8

University of Toronto Press acknowledges the financial assistance to its
publishing program of the Canada Council for the Arts and the Ontario Arts
Council, an agency of the Government of Ontario.

 Canada Council **Conseil des Arts**
for the Arts **du Canada**

ONTARIO ARTS COUNCIL
CONSEIL DES ARTS DE L'ONTARIO
an Ontario government agency
un organisme du gouvernement de l'Ontario

Funded by the   Financé par le
Government   gouvernement
of Canada   du Canada

This book is dedicated to my family, the center of my universe: My wife, Judy, and two children, Todd and Erica. I want to thank each one of you for your constant encouragement and feedback as I worked on the manuscript, and for sharing my passion for politics with me. This book would not have been written without your urging, Judy, so thank you.

Contents

Acknowledgments

This book is the result of the cooperation of several key people who worked with me at different stages of the project. First and foremost, I want to thank Jennifer DiDomenico, acquisitions editor, business and economics, of the University of Toronto Press. You were a constant source of insight at every stage of the development of this project, from the very first contact we had over the phone, to the many exchanges of detailed e-mails that ensued throughout the writing process. Your very high editorial standards pushed me to bring out my best as a thinker and writer, and proved to be invaluable as the book ebbed and flowed through many iterations. This book is the result of a very close collaboration between writer and editor, one that I have never before experienced in any of the previous books I have written, a process that has served to strengthen and crystallize the book's important message. In addition, I want to thank the rest of the editorial staff at the University of Toronto Press who worked with me during the later stages of the development of the book in their various capacities: Leah Connor (managing editor); Ani Deyirmenjian (production manager); Margaret Allen (copy editor); and Greg Devitt (design). Each of you, in your own capacity, contributed significantly to the development of the book.

I want to recognize the work of my assistants who carried out the detailed and necessary task of library research for this project. In particular, three of my graduate assistants in the Kellstadt Graduate School of Business at DePaul University worked very closely with me to generate a body of literature that was used as the foundation for each of the chapters: Dave Hevenor-Faulk, Dale Crawford, and Maria Uspenskaya. Each of you worked with me in a diligent and timely fashion to carry out extensive research to identify and accumulate the work of hundreds of scholars, political consultants, and journalists who covered, analyzed, and wrote about the recent U.S. presidential campaigns, especially the two elections in 2008 and 2012. I also want to thank Juan Lopez who worked in the Department of Marketing for helping me to carry out some of the more technical duties of pulling together the manuscript with figures and references, and setting up the files to submit to the publishing company.

This book is the result of a peer-review process that was critical to the development of the ideas that were shaped as the project moved through several different stages. The completed manuscript was reviewed by three anonymous scholars who were expert in different areas covered in the book. The book is an integration of several different disciplines, and the reviewers provided me with a very detailed critique that proved to be invaluable as the manuscript was edited and revised. I want to recognize my colleagues who either worked with me directly or who, through their own scholarship, helped me to shape the thinking that laid the foundation for several of the chapters in the book. These include: Andzrej Falkowski and Wojciech Cwalina of the Department of Marketing Psychology at the University of Social Sciences and Humanities in Warsaw, Poland, together with whom I have written articles, chapters, and books on the subject of political marketing that have advanced the theoretical development of the field over the past decade; Dennis Johnson, former acting director of the Graduate School of Political Management at George Washington University, who has written extensively on political consulting; Richard Perloff of the Department of Communication at Cleveland State University, who has contributed to the theoretical foundation of the field of political communication and to highlighting the importance of the role that political marketing plays in that discipline; and to those colleagues who have worked closely with me over the past fourteen years in my capacity as editor-in-chief of the *Journal of Political Marketing*: Christine Williams of the Department of Government at Bentley University (Managing Editor for North America); Dianne Dean of the Department of Marketing and Business Strategy at Hull University, United Kingdom (Managing Editor for Europe); Wayne Steger of the Department of Political Science at DePaul University (Associate Editor for North America); Dominic Wring of the Department of Political Communication at Loughborough University, United Kingdom (Associate Editor for Europe); and Paul Baines of the Department of Management at Cranfield University, United Kingdom (Associate Editor for Europe).

Last, but certainly not least, is my dedicated family from whom I took time away from personal activities on many occasions to lock myself in my office and work on this book. Judy, my wife, who is an artist, and shares the politics of her subject matter with me, thank you for sitting very patiently on many occasions as I bounced ideas and sentences of this book off you to get the reaction of someone who has become a very informed citizen of politics over the years from listening to me talk at length about the subject. Todd and Erica, I want to thank you both – as young professionals who understand the importance of politics as it shapes the fields you study and share with me, climate change (Todd) and sustainable management (Erica) – for your feedback on different thoughts I had about the subject of this book. Our conversations about the political implications that are connected to the environment offered me fresh insights on politics.

THE MARKETING REVOLUTION IN POLITICS

In both runs for the presidency, the Obama campaign determined early on that by using data to pinpoint voters with greater specificity, it could run its organization with better precision and efficiency. Instead of relying on the more traditional political and socio-demographic categories of voters, such as those who called themselves Democrats or liberals, Obama's marketing gurus instead relied on voter analytics to target political commercials and appeals to carefully defined segments of voters. This resulted in a promotional campaign that used big databases to cull information from voters' television viewing patterns to develop advertising appeals that they were confident would resonate with the desired audience. This same technology was used throughout the campaign to send requests for funds and volunteer support to social media sites that were frequented by voters who were most likely to support Obama. The revolution that took place during the Obama campaigns was the most advanced use of micro-targeting techniques that had ever been witnessed in a political campaign.

Who can forget the infamous Daisy commercial used by the incumbent Lyndon B. Johnson during the 1964 U.S. presidential campaign to sway voters away from his opponent? After the death of John F. Kennedy in 1963, Johnson took over as president and commander-in-chief, finding himself in a presidential campaign in 1964 against the Republican nominee, Barry Goldwater. Mr. Goldwater represented a hawkish view of the world, and the Johnson strategists decided to run a commercial with the intent of scaring voters into thinking that the United States would wind up in a nuclear war if Goldwater were elected. The commercial, which aired only once, used a little girl, who is seen picking petals from a flower, one by one, until she gets to the last petal, when a voice is heard counting down to a missile launch that ends in a nuclear explosion. The tactic convinced voters that Goldwater was a threat to the country and helped to win the election for Johnson in a landslide victory. This was a critical turning point in the history of political campaigns in the United States. Such a use of extreme, negative advertising to create fear in voters had never before been seen in any presidential campaign. At that time, television advertising was the "state of the art" in politics.

Fifty Years Later

Fifty years after the country watched in shock as the Daisy commercial used by Lyndon Johnson brought about one of the greatest landslide victories in the United States, American citizens would get another shock with the landslide victories of Barack Obama in 2008 and 2012. With only 270 Electoral College votes necessary to win the election, in 2008 Obama had 365 votes, and in 2012 he had 332. Further evidence of the power of the new marketing tools used in the campaigns is the fact that Obama won in 2012 with only slightly over 50 percent of the popular vote, a testament to his use of carefully targeted marketing efforts. By relying on the use of micro-targeting technology, and only focusing on the states where he knew he had a chance of winning by a small margin, in 2012 Obama was able to use his advertising dollars more effectively and efficiently than his opponent, Mitt Romney.

During the 2008 campaign, through the analysis of massive amounts of information that appeared on social media websites, the Obama strategists determined that millennials were attracted to Obama because of his fresh approach to politics and his promise to bridge the differences between Democrats and Republicans. The same type of research drove the thinking of Obama's strategists in 2012, as they worked to pull together a new coalition of voters that included younger people, Hispanics, single women, and African-Americans, all of whom may have voted for Obama because of policies he advocated, personality traits he possessed, or promises that resonated differently with each of the various segments of voters. For example, in an effort to target Hispanic voters, the Obama team in 2012 used nontraditional media outlets to reach them, relying on Spanish-speaking radio stations and sports radio shows. Obama also went out of his way to communicate with voters by using less politically oriented responses to radio journalists and speaking more about cultural issues that resonated with this audience. There are numerous other examples in the following chapters that demonstrate the sophisticated and creative use of marketing by campaign strategists.

Marketing in a Political Context

This book will report on a paradigm shift taking place in politics today that is affecting the business world. It will include case studies that analyze the successful application and execution of marketing innovations and strategies in the political marketplace, examples from which other sectors in society can learn. The book will rely on the analysis of recent U.S. presidential campaigns, with an emphasis on the Obama campaigns of 2008 and 2012, and, in some cases, will make reference to other classic campaigns of the past few decades. Political campaigns at the presidential level in the United States have become full-blown marketing campaigns with a reliance on and refinement of techniques found on the commercial side, all of which are used to better understand voters in an effort to strengthen the relationship between a candidate and citizens.

The movement toward building a stronger relationship with an organization's customers is an ongoing process for all business sectors. Take the Jewel-Osco chain of grocery stores, for example, where loyalty cards were eliminated in 2013 with the promise to customers that everyone would receive the same low prices. In an effort to maintain their contact with customers, Jewel created a new app for any shoppers who signed up for it and were willing to provide information about themselves. This reflected the company's attempt to build a one-to-one relationship with its customers through the popular and cost-effective use of digital coupons. In a similar vein, business organizations know well that it is more advantageous to target customers of cable television shows that attract niche viewers than to use traditional television outlets that charge as much as 100 times more to run the same thirty-second commercial.

Political operatives have borrowed these same techniques as a cheaper and more efficient way to identify and convince voters "sitting on the fence" to shift allegiance to their candidate. But because of the condensed nature of a presidential campaign, and the necessity to effectively create a start-up organization for every election, the political marketplace offers an example of the creative use of marketing strategies not found in any other sector.

For example, the 24/7 oversight of a presidential candidate's every word and action forces the campaign to be in crisis mode with a frequency not found in any other marketplace. The necessity to raise millions of dollars from so many diverse segments of contributors in such a short period puts pressure on a campaign to utilize the most sophisticated technological tools available to generate the donations that a nonprofit organization relies on to exist. For the first time in a U.S. presidential campaign, the use of data-mining techniques that merged databases containing voters' shopping patterns, television habits, and other voter characteristics enabled the Obama campaigns to more effectively target their advertising appeals and to alter them in real time to match the apparent preferences of the person navigating the web.

This book reports on a marketing revolution that has raised the bar on the use of standard marketing techniques – from following the marketing concept, to branding, advertising, and building relationships with customers – that continue to be used in business but are now part of a paradigm shift that has changed the way presidential campaigns are run. In doing so, the book also puts forward a blueprint for other organizations to follow, outlining seven marketing lessons, with a chapter devoted to each one, and with a focus on the Obama Model, analyzing how his campaign relied on creative marketing solutions to win in each of his two runs for the presidency. Each chapter then extrapolates the lesson to both for-profit and nonprofit organizations that rely on the same methods to succeed in their respective marketplaces, while highlighting the differences among these contexts.

The book shows how the methods used by corporations like Disney, Google, IBM, and Procter & Gamble are also used by entities like the U.S. government and the Pope. The book will be of great interest to marketing managers, MBA students, and general readers wishing to learn more about how President Obama was able to mastermind Electoral College victories in two presidential campaigns by winning by the smallest of margins in battleground states. The book highlights both the actors and their strategies in each of the 2008 and 2012 campaigns. Every organization is constantly trying not only to maintain relationships with existing customers and attract competitors' customers in an effort to maintain and increase their market share, but also to understand how to attract customers who may have very different reasons for using the same product or service. Ultimately, this challenge calls for the use of innovative marketing strategies to arrive at one central theme that appeals to very different segments of customers. The genius of the Obama Model lies in its use of the most innovative and cost-effective marketing tactics to accomplish these goals.

So What Is Political Marketing?

Politicians are effectively service providers, promising to offer benefits to citizens and voters in all political parties. They are engaged in a constant struggle to hang onto the voters who put them into office and to find ways of attracting new voters as one campaign cycle leads to another. The need to constantly innovate is an imperative for any successful organization; it must constantly search for more effective and efficient ways of understanding customers' needs and wants and for better approaches to maintaining a relationship with them.

These imperatives are equally applicable to any manager who sells products. Whereas a service is offered by a person, a product is a tangible item. It can be marketed in different ways through standardization and production technologies that are used to communicate with and deliver goods to people. Just as Obama learned to use marketing to establish his image as a consistent and steady leader, so product-oriented companies can learn to use marketing to establish the image of their products in the marketplace by emphasizing particular attributes.

There is a common consensus that political marketing is extremely important to various functions of democracies. These include but are not limited to: elections, referenda, governing, lobbying, and public services management. Political marketing represents the triumph of an approach that first originated in business and then transformed the nature of modern politics. So, any company, individual, or organization engaged in trying to win over customers (all corporations); influence the thinking of government officials (lobbyists); or simply influence public opinion (political action committees, interest groups, nonprofit organizations) will be interested in the lessons put forward in this book.

The use of marketing in politics today is omnipresent, a part of every campaign, from local school board elections all the way up to presidential campaigns. The level of sophistication and amount of money spent will naturally be greater in presidential elections, which also represent the most interesting and complex application of marketing. This book focuses on the presidential level in an effort to highlight examples that will have the most meaning to organizations that operate in other sectors in society, including those in the nonprofit and for-profit sectors. Anecdotes about incidents and events in each of the Obama campaigns will be highlighted to make the case for the innovative use of marketing.

For example, looking back at the 2012 campaign, who could forget the incident at the Republican National Convention when Clint East-wood addressed an empty chair that was meant to represent President Obama? In what many would identify as a mini-crisis moment for the Obama team, there was a hi-tech response by the President; he sent out a tweet on an account set up immediately, and within minutes destroyed the impact of the whole affair with an online picture of the President in a chair at the White House, accompanied by a clever quip ("This seat's taken …"), making light of the gesture by Mr. Eastwood. Unlike other marketplaces that can operate without a constant 24/7 laser beam on every move made by the CEO, the political marketplace is one in which strategists must be ready with tactical responses to negative advertising attacks that can take place at any time. In addition to highlighting the use of marketing as a campaign tool, I will also examine how it is used by a sitting president to try to drive public opinion in a desired direction – what has been referred to as the permanent campaign.[1]

Politics Today

For many years now, marketing techniques and strategies have been imported into politics to help candidates win office and create an op-portunity for political organizations, both inside and outside govern-ment, to influence the decision-making political elite (in this book, in Washington, D.C.).[2] In the past few decades, politicians and their advisors have become ever more sophisticated in using management and marketing strategies to influence a marketplace that is much more highly regulated and scrutinized than most commercial arenas. Poli-ticians today must be ready to react to a wide range of competition, including but not limited to other candidates, political action commit-tees, special interest groups, and a whole host of organizations and in-dividuals who seek to drive public opinion on certain issues and for certain causes. During the course of a presidential campaign, this some-times takes place instantaneously, which is very much the result of a "horse-race" mentality that develops as the campaign goes forward. Furthermore, the role of negative advertising has become a fixture in contemporary politics, exacerbating the crisis mentality that already exists in most election campaigns.[3]

Political organizations now face problems similar to those found on the commercial side, and vice-versa. Simultaneous with the running of the marketing campaign is the financial campaign. The latter may possibly usurp and take over the political campaign as political organizations report fund-raising levels that reflect the popularity of a candidate; in some cases it may doom a campaign, when there seems to be no interest, or it may be used to intimidate candidates who do not think they can match the funds raised by the leading contender in a race. Political organizations must rely on sophisticated marketing strategies to stay financially viable over the course of a campaign cycle. In an interesting twist, the notion of the vigilante citizen, a scourge of politicians who support issues that upset citizens organized in political action committees and issues groups, has now made its way into the commercial marketplace, where consumers not happy with a company's actions are able to voice their concerns through social media in a manner resembling political protest. To put it another way, the commercial marketplace is becoming very political.

Every political campaign must also rely on the effective use of public relations. However, unlike in a public relations campaign for a commercial product or service, political public relations people have to work harder because there are so many different constituencies to be contacted. As the American public ages, the average age of the evening news watcher is rising; it becomes more of a challenge for political operatives to get out their message to age cohorts that may not get their information from old-line media outlets.[4]

A revolution of sorts has taken place in politics, with political parties and individual political candidates realizing that they cannot succeed in politics without the use of marketing. There is a continual reliance on the use of money to fuel marketing campaigns to put out the constant barrage of commercials required to brand and rebrand the images and platforms of candidates and their opponents. It has become very apparent that politics in the United States is dependent on marketing campaigns that do not even remotely resemble Harry Truman's whistle-stop campaign in 1948, in which he delivered stump speeches to voters at selected stops around the country.

A Unique Case Study

The application of marketing to politics, especially at the presidential level, offers a unique research opportunity. Several challenges exist with the marketing of a president. First of all, in a presidential campaign, there is the need to reach out to many different segments of voters, each of whom may prefer a particular candidate but for very different reasons. Some voters cast a ballot for a candidate because of the issues and policies the candidate stands for; others because of the candidate's promise to change things if elected; others because of their association with different groups of supporters; and still others because they are convinced that the candidate will make their lives better. All share a belief that it makes sense to vote for this person based on a hope that the candidate will keep his or her promises. Compare this decision-making process with that of typical BMW automobile owners, who probably know exactly what they are getting when they buy a car – a luxurious vehicle that offers them high performance and projects an image of success. The point here is that there will not likely be any surprises when they drive the car home. This is very different from casting a ballot for a candidate because of a strong movement of popular support, as happened with Barack Obama in 2008, where a momentum built up that swept voters off their feet with an emotional high that is unique to politics.

Second, the preferences of voters are constantly changing as new issues and circumstances present new challenges to the candidate trying to market a campaign platform based on the status-quo thinking of a political party rather than the thinking of a maverick candidate who sees things differently. The pressure of constantly shifting events – whether the threat of a foreign enemy who is bent on bringing about havoc in the United States, or an economy on the brink of collapse – heightens voter volatility and makes the marketing of a presidential candidate very difficult. In short, there is a world of difference between the voter and the typical BMW automobile owner; in all likelihood, the latter has a very firm understanding of the product characteristics, and when one aggregates this across all BMW owners, there is probably a very consistent set of attributes that buyers look for in this car, even as new models are brought out from year to year.

Third, a range of forces impinge on and make it very difficult to operate in the political marketplace with any sense of control. In effect, a presidential campaign is in a constant state of crisis from the moment it begins, without resolution until the election is over. The forces may come from within or outside the country, but the one constant is that they are often unknown until they hit the news. This requires politicians to constantly reposition their image and appeals in an effort to keep their poll numbers high. This constant repositioning is not going to be as drastic for the BMW corporation, as its position as a premier automobile company is a constant. Further complicating the political marketplace is the use of these same methods after a candidate wins office in an effort to keep his or her poll numbers high while running the country. A sitting president may need to make one or two critical decisions daily, as compared to a CEO of a corporation who likely needs to make one or two critical decisions once a month.[5]

Fourth, media campaigns in a presidential contest can be very vicious and full of negativity, raising issues that constantly put candidates on the defensive, and, if the negative attack is effective, preventing them from putting out a positive message. This is not the case for BMW, which may only find itself on the receiving end of a negative media campaign if there is a problem with a new model or some manufacturing defect that calls for a public relations campaign to quell the media frenzy.

Perhaps one of the most interesting characteristics of a U.S. presidential campaign is the fact that there are two major political parties, whose adherents tend to stay loyal to their respective nominees, contending for the support of the relatively few voters who are sitting on the fence, not sure whom they want to vote for. The major effort that needs to be made strategically and tactically, then, is keeping the party loyalists happy while responding to the issues that the fence-sitters are looking to hear candidates talk about. This is a very different challenge than the one BMW faces, where the level of loyalty may not be as great as one finds in politics, with many car buyers looking to buy a new model every five to seven years. By contrast, candidates who represent a party will find it very difficult to get voters to switch their party allegiance, mainly due to the strong ideological differences that exist between the two parties.

Several but not all of the major characteristics that distinguish the political market from other marketplaces have been identified. In the chapters that follow, the uniqueness of this case study will become more apparent, with specific reference to the topic of each chapter. It will become obvious that the challenges faced by a politician often eclipse the challenges faced by a marketing manager in the nonprofit or for-profit sector, or, in some interesting twists that will become clear, there may be challenges in nonpolitical sectors that call for even more creative marketing thinking.

Take the task of having to raise funds for a nonprofit organization that does not have the celebrity status of a Barack Obama or Bill Clinton and that is working hard to get someone to donate in an effort to keep the nonprofit alive. How can other organizations learn from the lessons of the recent Obama campaigns, which were brilliant at getting citizens to contribute millions of dollars? For example, in one very successful campaign, the Obama strategists determined that there was a great interest among some key segments of voters in meeting and having dinner with celebrities like George Clooney and Sarah Jessica Parker. Relying on the use of micro-targeting efforts, the campaign identified voters who fitted a specific demographic profile and contacted them through the Internet. The result was a very successful fund-raising campaign, one of several that will be reported on later in the book.

Obama's two campaigns in particular provide evidence of how marketing can be applied to a nonbusiness setting that incorporates many of the same ingredients one would find in a typical marketplace in which a firm sells various products and services to customers. In fact, his two campaigns closely resemble some of the many start-ups that are popping up in industries around the globe, where entrepreneurs familiar with the latest technological advances are able to target niche markets with their new products and services. With the myriad changes taking place in the world of politics, and specifically in the way campaigns are run, the opportunity exists for students of other markets to borrow and learn from the recent Obama campaigns, applying these insights to a dynamic business setting that is full of uncertainties and crises, and using data-gathering techniques to acquire the necessary intelligence to respond effectively to them.

Political campaigns continue to spend huge amounts of money to market candidates, with hundreds of millions of dollars being spent on political campaigns at the presidential level. The book will highlight the importance of following the marketing concept to identify the needs and wants of key constituencies in the marketplace, including government, the media, consumers, and other key publics. Just as a political campaign is not an island unto itself, but must operate in a world where public opinion is shaped by many different influences, so must corporations learn to deal with multiple publics and adapt their strategy to the realities of the changing mood of their customers.

Merging the Worlds of Politics and Business

The two successful Obama campaigns (especially the one in 2012) introduced a whole new set of electioneering tactics that can be used to win over customers in any marketplace. For example, Obama redefined how to go about identifying who your potential customers are. Voters who had not cast a ballot previous to the 2012 U.S. presidential election were convinced to do so. At the same time, Obama used innovative methods to encourage repeat voting behavior among supporters from 2008 – some of them reluctant. All types of organizations are always trying to find new customers and at the same time hold onto those they already have. The Obama operatives revealed how they were able to attract millions of dollars using e-mail technology that had been refined through extensive experimentation. For example, when they embarked on fund-raising campaigns, they tried out many different phrases in the subject line of an e-mail to potential donors to determine the exact wording that would attract the greatest response.

Just as unforeseen events shape the commercial marketplace, so do they shape political campaigns, and, in fact, may cause them to turn in an instant. Political campaigns are always subject to the ebb and flow of unforeseen events, including lackluster performances by candidates at critical moments that can play a key role in moving the candidate's poll numbers. If you think back to the 2012 campaign, there were many critical events that seemed to turn the tide both for and against each of the two candidates. Whether it was a verbal gaffe by one of the candidates (Romney's "47 percent" comment) or a poor showing in a debate (Obama in the first debate), each of the respective organizations saw its poll numbers drop very quickly at different points in the campaign. No other marketplace will see its sales figures drop as precipitously as in politics.

Rebranding a product or service, or even an entire organization that finds itself viewed in an unfavorable light in the media, is not a simple marketing challenge, and calls for new and different ways to communicate with customers from varied backgrounds. At the heart of a communication strategy for any organization is a brand identity that enables it to rise above any claims that seek to redefine the company in a negative light. During both of his victorious campaigns, Obama was able to create a brand strategy that had equity with voters from very different backgrounds. This was accomplished through the innovative use of carefully crafted logos, consistent use of the same colors and designs on all campaign posters and in all campaign commercials, and the use of media for different purposes.

The definition of a candidate's brand very much ties into the logo that is developed to provide a visual representation of the future direction in which the leader will take the country. This is no different than the use of the "golden arches" by McDonald's to define its brand. During the 2008 campaign, Obama promised to bring a new culture to Washington. This was accomplished with a picture that represented the sun rising over the horizon, signifying the promise of hope to the citizens, and using the colors of red, white, and blue to suggest that his campaign was built on a patriotic foundation. In 2012, although there were elements of the 2008 logo used, especially as they tied into the issues of the campaign, the tagline in 2012 was "For Leadership We Can Believe In," an echo of the tagline in 2008, "Change We Can Believe In." Obama relied on similar versions of his 2008 logo, as it was clearly a successful visual of his message for hope and new horizons.

Another facet of the political marketplace that will resonate with all organizations is the way in which employees of a political organization are made to feel part of a movement. For example, all organizations will be in a better position to educate employees by indoctrinating them with an ideology that they agree with and are able to advance themselves; similarly, a big factor in political success is having a philosophy that is shared by all members of a party. Yes, all organizations have members, too, called employees, with a connection that may bond them in a different way because of the use of money to pay for their services, but it will become apparent that the use of nonmonetary methods to motivate team members is often even more effective because it relies on the use of emotion to drive people's behavior.

In some cases, the development of a movement (such as the Tea Party on the Republican side) creates an almost cult-like following that makes persuasive messages even more effective when they are couched in the language of the movement's leader. This is part of the branding process in politics, and it is not uncommon in some cases to see the same on the commercial side, when consumers are so strongly connected to the products they use that it plays out in a similar fashion – examples include those professionals who meet on Sundays in the summer months to ride their Harley-Davidson motorcycles as part of a movement of bikers, or users of Android smartphones who favor the same technology for the watches they put on their wrist or the glasses they put on their face.

With the necessity of attracting voters from both major political parties in any run for the presidency, a presidential candidate needs to rely on the marketing lessons reported in this book to identify new and creative ways to appeal to voters beyond the party faithful. Perhaps the most significant challenge for a political organization is the necessity of attracting voters from the opposing party. A political party cannot rely solely on voters in one party to win an election. Similarly, the marketers of any product or service need to constantly attract customers from their competitors as it becomes harder to hold onto existing customers. In effect, political campaigns need to reach out to a wide spectrum of voters in the same way that some organizations seek to attract customers who use their product or services for very different reasons. Smart marketers find ways to sell their offerings to diverse customers – what is referred to in the marketing discipline as market segmentation. The imperative in a presidential political campaign is to carry out this tactic to a degree that is beyond the scope of most organizations by finding new and different ways to accomplish the goal.

Politics Rises to a New Level of Technological Sophistication

For many years, politics has relied on the use of commercial marketing methods to "sell" politicians to voters; recently, however, these methods have reached a new level of sophistication because of the use of the latest technological advances in political campaigns. For example, one of the most fundamental axioms in the field of marketing is that organizations must first identify the needs and wants of their customers before they can successfully sell their products and services to them. What has happened over the past several years is the introduction of micro-targeting by organizations to pinpoint the needs and wants of individual customers through the sophisticated use of Big Data. The Obama campaigns engaged in a significant amount of data-mining by integrating different databases to identify profiles of critical voter segments. This was accomplished in part by integrating the television habits of voters, along with their shopping habits, and any other characteristics that could help to profile them, and using that information to help the campaign's advertising strategists more effectively target voters with attractive and meaningful appeals.

It has become a common practice in organizations across many different industries to develop advertising campaigns that rely on the use of customer analytics to alter an appeal used on a website in real time on the basis of the profile of the person who is navigating the web. Maintaining and building relationships with customers today now requires the use of social media to keep the contact between the organization and its customers alive. In addition, crises that arise in any organization must be carefully managed on social media to ensure that they do not go viral, or, if they do, to minimize the negative impact on the reputation of the company. The use of the latest technological tools to shape the tactics and strategy of successful political campaigns is part of the marketing revolution in politics that this book reports on.

This is not to suggest that the standard marketing methods that have evolved over the past sixty years are not still in play in politics, as well as in the nonprofit and for-profit worlds. It is only to suggest that the successful application of marketing today must incorporate these latest methods in new and creative ways, a fact that will become clearer as the reader compares and contrasts how organizations use market segmentation, product positioning, advertising campaigns, and other marketing tools to implement successful marketing strategies. All organizations still rely on these methods in unique ways that reflect on the characteristics of the marketplaces they operate in. In the political world, the use of marketing has evolved over the past sixty years into a thriving academic field that has stimulated growth in the consulting world, enabling it to reap the profits from understanding and applying these methods.[6]

The Gradual Shift in Politics

The movement in politics from a focus on the party concept (which emphasizes the importance and role of the political party) to the marketing concept (which in a political campaign establishes the importance of understanding voter needs and wants before proceeding to the development of a campaign platform) is in great part due to a decline in the number of people who consider themselves partisans and an increase in the number who consider themselves independents. Along with this shift has come the importance of zeroing in on and spending advertising dollars on marketing the political candidate as opposed to the party, where different candidates offer different leadership styles within the same political party. This mirrors the evolution that takes place in many markets, with a shift from a manufacturing or production focus toward a focus on selling and, eventually, marketing. For example, take the case of the Model T Ford (which was offered in only one color – black), where the emphasis was on the research and development of the automobile and the innovative methods used to produce it, an approach soon imitated and then refined by competitors like General Motors, who began to focus on customers who sought out an automobile produced in different styles and different colors.[7]

In an election, the "political product" is the campaign platform. It consists of several elements, including: (1) the general election program of the candidate based on the political and economic guidelines of the party he or she belongs to or the organization set up for the time of the elections; (2) the candidate's positions on the most important problems highlighted during the campaign; (3) the candidate's image; (4) the candidate's connection to a particular political background and groups of supporters (e.g., labor unions, associations, NGOs) or authorities. Such a platform is flexible and evolves together with the development of the voting campaign and changes in the voting situation.[8]

Theory development in political marketing has borrowed from several different social science disciplines over the past several decades. At the very heart of this pursuit is the understanding of human behavior that encompasses the various activities involved in political marketing. The sum total of those activities is put forward in the following definition: Political marketing is based on "the applications of marketing principles and procedures in political campaigns by various individuals and organizations. The procedures involved include the analysis, development, execution and management of strategic campaigns by candidates, political parties, governments, lobbyists and interest groups that seek to drive public opinion, advance their own ideologies, win elections and pass legislation and referenda in response to the needs and wants of selected people and groups in society."[9]

The use of marketing methods by political organizations has brought about a discussion over the past few decades that centers on the similarities and differences between marketing a politician or political party and marketing other products (e.g., soap, automobiles) and services (e.g., medical, legal). For example, whereas the same methods that were used during the Obama campaigns are certainly being used by companies selling products, the better and more accurate application of these methods comes closer to those used by individuals or companies selling a service to customers. Applying mainstream marketing to politics has been justified by several similarities and differences that I will now elaborate on.[10]

If one were to compare the purchase of a bar of soap to voting, the first distinction between that and voting is that the consumption of soap does not require nearly as much time and effort for a consumer in choosing one brand over another as does deciding to cast a ballot for a candidate. As a result, a buyer of soap will be less involved in the acquisition of information than a voter is. Second, taking note that a candidate is really a service provider makes the distinction between campaigning and governing clearer. The actual delivery of a service that a candidate offers to the voter does not occur until he or she begins to govern. Finally, candidates operate in a dynamic environment, fast changing and full of obstacles that present marketing challenges that require flexibility and agility on the part of the politician. Just as corporations around the world must alter their services in response to a more demanding consumer in the commercial marketplace, so candidates have to respond to the fast-paced changes that take place in the political marketplace.

Some further distinctions that separate political marketing from product marketing are as follows: services are intangible, meaning that there is not an exchange of a physical product; a service is by definition variable, meaning it can be good on some days and bad on others; it is perishable, which is to say it is consumed instantaneously and cannot be stored; and finally, one cannot separate the provider of the service from the production of the offering. Each of these service distinctions applies to a candidate during the course of an election, or to a politician who is in the midst of running a government.

As service providers, all politicians are making promises to voters on a regular basis. The point here is to make, fulfill, and enable all promises that are communicated to an audience. Just as a company is always concerned with making promises to attract new customers, so is the politician. However, it is not enough to make the promises to build relationships; it is also necessary to deliver on them.

The fact that there are many similarities between political marketing and mainstream marketing (product, service, not-for-profit, and relationship) does not in itself justify linking the two disciplines. To get a better understanding of the use of marketing in politics, one needs to take a closer look at the differences between mainstream and political marketing. For example, in business, the ultimate goal is financial success, whereas in politics it is strengthening democracy through voting processes. Using various marketing strategies in economic practice is the result of conducting market research that promises satisfactory financial profits. In politics, on the other hand, a candidate's own philosophy often influences the scope of marketing strategies. This means that although marketing research may suggest that a politician's chances will increase if he or she concentrates on particular political or economic issues, the candidate does not have to follow these suggestions if his or her own conception of political reality is incongruent with these issues.

The main imperative in marketing ultimately rests on the concept of a transaction that takes place between a company offering products and services to customers in exchange for their loyalty to the company.[11] When applying marketing to politics, the transaction centers on a candidate who offers political leadership in exchange for a vote from the citizen. When voters cast their ballots, they are engaged in an exchange of time and support (their vote) for the services the party/candidate offers, after the election, through better government. The emphasis on the processes of election exchanges cannot obscure the fact that political marketing is not limited only to the period of the election campaign. In the era of the permanent campaign, in reality there is no clear difference between the period directly before the election and the rest of the political calendar. Governing to and through endless campaigns eventually establishes a politician's credibility. This brings us to another well-accepted definition of political marketing: it is "the processes of exchanges and establishing, maintaining, and enhancing relationships among objects in the political market (politicians, political parties, voters, interests groups, institutions), whose goal is to identify and satisfy their needs and develop political leadership."[12]

It is now virtually impossible to win political office in the United States without the support of a staff of strategists, including pollsters, advertising experts, social media technology experts, and other people who all come together to form an organization that gets up and running and operates as a mini-organization with the goal of getting a candidate elected to office. This is true for people running for positions as trustees in villages around the country, all the way up to candidates seeking the highest office in the country, the presidency. There are both obvious and more subtle parallels between the political, for-profit, and nonprofit worlds; as they continue to evolve, the similarities and differences in strategy and tactics in all three sectors need to be analyzed in a comparative manner that sheds light on the innovative use of marketing in each sector while also clarifying why the word "revolution" was used in the title of this book.

An Emphasis on Tactics as Opposed to Strategy

The case of the political campaign put forward in this book will resonate with middle-level managers who seek to understand how best to act on a day-to-day basis in an effort to achieve long-term success in their organization. This calls for the merging of and inter-connectedness between strategy and tactics. So perhaps it is prudent at this point to define the difference between the two. Strategy provides a set of broad goals for an organization to follow in an effort to achieve long-term success. There are several questions that should be considered when goals are established. These include what it is an organization wants to achieve; by what date they want it achieved; why they want to achieve the goal(s); what they need to do to carry out the goals; the identification and allocation of resources that will enable them to achieve their goals; and finally the understanding of factors both inside the organization and in the environment that could impact on those goals. Tactics then are defined as the action that needs to take place to help achieve the strategy – or, alternatively, as sub-goals necessary to ensure that the goals support the mission of the organization. At the heart of the message of this book is the proposition that both strategy and tactics must always begin with an understanding of your customers' needs and wants.[13]

As we take a closer look at the world of politics, particularly at the role of strategy and tactics during the course of a political campaign, we can identify similar characteristics in the commercial sector, where organizations succeed by identifying the needs and wants of their targeted customers and creating a long-term relationship with them. In politics, the same principle holds true – to meet the needs and wants of voters in elections. However, in politics, there is a unique circumstance that includes the employment of consultants whose sole occupation is to use whatever information is necessary to create and re-create reality so a candidate's message can get out. The person who does this has been referred to as the "spin doctor." The reality is, as data suggest, that business organizations which use a marketing strategy centering on an ethical orientation are normally more successful than organizations that do not. This of course raises the issue of negative advertising in politics and the impact it has on the "customer" base, namely voters. There needs to be a continuing effort on the part of actors in the political world to adopt this model.[14]

What does tend to happen when new technologies are merged with consumer research is that it is difficult for companies to increase the number of interactions with their customer base. According to data from the 2012 Accenture Global Consumer Pulse, only 15 percent of customers are satisfied with the service programs of the firms they work with, and a full 47 percent are actually frustrated that the companies they do business with have not taken the time to use the information forwarded to them concerning complaints they may have had. The net result is that approximately 80 percent of customers have indicated that they have considered switching companies as a result of the dissatisfaction that they encountered. What has been recommended to deal with this situation is the merging of strategy with more current tactics – specifically, that customer complaints be dealt with in a timely manner, with realistic expectations customized to the form of information and communication outlet that a particular customer is comfortable with. The point is that everything should be done to bring tactics in line with strategy to keep customers happy and loyal.[15]

Ultimately, in order for tactics to be most effective, regardless of the strategy they are used with, organizations must make an effort to be actively responsive to the customer and to focus on the actual experience of the customer. There should also be an effort to use tactics from any competitor who is successful in other sectors, whether they are in business or politics, even if it means completely re-inventing the core business a company is in.[16]

Plan of the Book

To establish the connection between marketing and politics, chapter 1 takes the reader through presidential campaigns over the past sixty years that reveal how marketing has evolved and has been used in successive presidential campaigns. The historical foundation for the marketing revolution in politics this book reports on will be established in this chapter, as the reader is introduced to various tools and the actors who relied on them to win previous campaigns, going as far back as the presidential campaign of Dwight Eisenhower in 1952, and bringing the reader through to the 2012 campaign of President Barack Obama. The reader is introduced to the Strategic Triad, which is a visual representation of the latest technological innovations (referred to earlier in this chapter) that are now part of all political campaigns. The chapter ends with the introduction of the Obama Model, which represents the latest manifestation of the technological advances used by Obama in the 2008 and 2012 campaigns.

All marketing strategies begin with the basic understanding of the marketplace and the needs and wants of your customers (see chapter 2 – Lesson 1: Follow the Marketing Concept). This is then followed by the use of technological advances (chapter 3 – Lesson 2: Use Technology Strategically) and extensive marketing research (chapter 4 – Lesson 3:

Integrate Research Methods) to confirm, adapt, and refine the mixture of products and services that are offered to the public. Chapter 5 (Lesson 4: Develop a Unique Brand Identity) discusses the establishment of a brand that ties together all of the products and services offered to the public. Chapter 6 (Lesson 5: Create a Winning Advertising Strategy) covers the development of a promotional campaign strategy that will communicate the essence of the brand to targeted segments. Once the link with the targeted customers is established, it must be maintained and nurtured through the appropriate media channels and the building of long-term relationships (chapter 7 – Lesson 6: Build a Relationship with Your Customers). We live in a chaotic and unpredictable world, and for companies to be successful, they must be prepared to respond to crises (chapter 8 – Lesson 7: Be Prepared to Engage in Crisis Management). Finally, chapter 9 (Concluding Remarks) summarizes the lessons from the Obama Model, and looks ahead to the future use of marketing in the political, for-profit, and nonprofit sectors.

Chapter One

The Evolution of Marketing in Politics

To understand the innovative use of marketing in politics, we need to examine the introduction of modern marketing techniques in presidential campaigns that date back to the 1950s. It has now been over sixty years since Dwight D. Eisenhower used television advertising in his 1952 presidential campaign, the first time the medium was used in U.S. politics. Up until then, candidates relied on other media of their time, whether the printed newspaper or radio. Eight years later, the American public would witness the first real mass media campaign, culminating in the election of John F. Kennedy. Prior to 1960, mass media campaigns in the United States were used almost exclusively by corporations for selling commercial products and services.

From a historical point of view, the 1960 campaign, which pitted John F. Kennedy against Richard Nixon, was considered the beginning of the introduction of modern marketing techniques in presidential contests.[1] However, that is not to say that there were not technological innovations introduced into politics before 1960. In 1935, George Gallup left academia and formed his own polling company, called the American Institute of Public Opinion, which would become the base of operations for his Gallup Poll. In 1936, Gallup's company and his poll won national prominence by correctly predicting that Franklin D. Roosevelt would defeat Alf Landon, a prediction accomplished by polling only 50,000 people. This was in striking contrast to the poll run by the *Literary Digest* magazine that incorrectly predicted that Alf Landon would win on the basis of 2 million voters. A new era was ushered in with this technology, making it possible now to get accurate predictions of the results of an election weeks before it took place. After George Gallup started his company, Lou Harris would follow in 1956 with his polling firm, Louis Harris and Associates, and would become the first "official" presidential pollster, working with John F. Kennedy and helping to defeat Richard Nixon, in part on the basis of the application of his expertise to a presidential campaign.[2]

The 1960 presidential campaign was the first of several campaigns that were documented in books by Theodore H. White, who described and depicted the beginning of a paradigm shift in politics. White wrote in great detail about how John F. Kennedy was promoted using the most advanced technology available to political strategists. That campaign would also mark the start of a stronger emphasis on the candidate instead of the political party, and would bring into the political equation the understanding of branding and a focus on the characteristics of the presidential nominee's personality as a way to communicate with the American public. Up until that time in U.S. politics, presidential candidates represented political parties, and elections were conducted with an emphasis on party loyalty and the solicitation of support from citizens who would identify themselves as either Democrat or a Republican. That is not to suggest that citizens don't make that identification today, but it was the overwhelming basis on which a president was chosen during that era. The campaign in 1960 was the first one in which a presidential campaign spent as much money and effort in trying to sell voters a political candidate as in promoting a political party. This was the real beginning of the marketing revolution. As will be reported later in this chapter, this marketing revolution would continue on with successive candidacies over the following fifty years, bringing us up to the presidential campaign of Barack Obama in 2012.

The Beginning of Direct Mail in Politics

The critical point here is that many of the innovations and changes that have taken place over the past fifty years were based on and borrowed from methods used by corporate America, a testing ground for the latest tools used in a continuous effort to better understand the consumer in the commercial marketplace in order to keep customers loyal and prevent them from switching to a competitor. This is especially true for the technological advances of the 1970s and beyond. As the advances in marketing were carried over to the political world, more and more money was spent on the various component parts of the marketing effort to maintain a competitive position in a politician's attempt to win office. This included more money being spent on research, advertising, volunteer activities to get out the vote, and management techniques to control the ever-expanding number of consultants and strategists who became part of bigger and bigger campaign organizations.

The 1970s would lead to more sophisticated methods in direct marketing that Richard Viguerie, founder of *Conservative Digest* magazine in 1975 and a strong supporter of conservative causes, brought to bear. Viguerie brought sophisticated fund-raising techniques to the political marketplace, making it possible for presidential candidates, as well as candidates at all levels of office, to raise the many millions of dollars necessary to pay for the services of the wide range of experts who ran the marketing campaigns of the candidates using direct mail.

Polls Take on a New Sophistication

The polling carried out by Pat Cadell during Jimmy Carter's run for the presidency in 1976 introduced politics to the more advanced methods used in the commercial marketplace, connecting issues and voter segments into a database that was mined to analyze the electorate in an effort to target different issues to different groups. This was an advance over what Lou Harris had done for John Kennedy, as it relied on marketing research methods that went beyond simple predictions of who was most likely to support a candidate with an explanation behind why that support existed, whether because of the image of the candidate or the issues the politician stood for. In the case of Jimmy Carter, for the first time in many years, a southern politician would be marketed as "new and different" from the more traditional politician. The strategy worked, and it put Mr. Carter into the White House in 1976.

The 1970s also brought to politics Madison Avenue advertising expertise to manage the commercials that were run on television as the country went through an era where political campaigns for the presidency were conducted over the television airwaves. Advances in advertising and promotion were carried over from Madison Avenue in New York to Washington, D.C., by the likes of people such as H.R. Haldeman, whom Nixon brought into his campaign to manage putting out the message and, after winning the White House, into his inner cabinet as chief of staff. Haldeman did not have any experience in promoting anything other than commercial products and services, but having been active in Republican Party affairs previous to that, he proved to be quite capable of making the leap to political advertising advisor, and helped to successfully promote Richard Nixon, while breaking laws that would eventually put him into jail along with other Nixon aides who got caught in the Watergate scandal.

The Great Communicator

The political campaigns of Ronald Reagan in the 1980s would usher into politics an emphasis never before seen on the role of branding and communication, helped to a great degree by public relations expert Michael Deaver. Mr. Deaver understood the importance of consistency in message and backdrop as a way to create a brand identity for a politician. For example, Deaver made sure that all visual communications between Ronald Reagan and the American public always included an American flag in the background, helping to secure the image of Reagan as a strong patriot who pushed to strengthen American influence around the world, with the goal of dismantling of the Soviet Union. The method worked in large part because Mr. Reagan, a consummate actor, was able to play the "role" of loyal leader in command who promised to bring prestige back to the American landscape after the debacle of the Carter presidency with its miserable failure in the Iran hostage crisis. Branding Reagan was possible because he was a person who could be effectively marketed in this fashion.

The War Room and Permanent Campaign

The techniques developed in the 1990s brought the world of politics yet another step closer to where we are today. With the advances made by the Clinton campaigns in both 1992 and 1996, especially with the use of the "War Room," the high-tech nerve center of the 1992 Clinton campaign headquarters, the world of politics became more like what many would say was an organization run like a corporation but selling a candidate – Bill Clinton – rather than a product or service. Included in this new kind of political organization were technical experts who were adept at integrating all forms of communications technology to stay a step ahead of their competition. This included using faxes, telephones, and other methods both to send out messages to media to announce new policies and to respond to any charge leveled against their candidate before it became a story that could not be dealt with. (This was a lesson learned from the horrific collapse of the Dukakis campaign in the 1988 race against George H. Bush, where Bush consistently bashed Dukakis without any response, causing a drop in Dukakis's polls that he never recovered from.) The Clinton camp was determined to bring into their effort the likes of James Carville, known by many in the political world to be a very effective strategist.

The Clinton White House would also introduce the political world to what has been referred to as the "permanent campaign" – the post-election use of the same methods employed during the campaign – with many of his campaign advisors following him into the White House as senior presidential aides.[3] The Clinton White House incorporated more advanced methods in marketing from the commercial world that gave Clinton the ability to manage crises on a day-to-day basis with a clarity of message and a sharp focus, using what is referred to in the marketing world as target marketing, matching the message with the intended audience.

Negative Advertising Rises to a New Height

The Bush victories in 2000 and 2004 brought in the expertise of Karl Rove, a "numbers" person who was able to use mathematics to determine exactly how many votes were necessary to win an election. Rove also understood the ability to kill a competitor's campaign by airing television commercials over and over again to destroy the image of a politician. A case in point was the use of the Swift Boat commercials, which portrayed the Democratic candidate, John Kerry, as a person who had fabricated his own image as a hero, when instead he had let down his troops. Many have labeled this "negative advertising," now a permanent staple of American politics. The strategic initiatives of Karl Rove continued to be felt in the Republican Party as his political action committee, American Crossroads, sought to influence the political campaigns of Republican candidates from states around the country after he left the Bush White House, relying on similar tactics to influence results in campaigns that have had strategic influence on the success of the Republican Party.[4]

All of the presidential campaigns over the past sixty years up until the Obama victories in 2008 and 2012 relied on a successful application of business methods, as they advanced from decade to decade, each either introducing a new variation on an existing theme (such as the more advanced use of polling by Carter in 1976 over that of Kennedy in 1960) or an altogether new business application (such as the early 1970s use of direct mail by Republican Richard Viguerie to solicit funds and support). What did not happen, however, at any point over the past sixty years, was the use of business methods so innovative and advanced from previous presidential cycles that it could be called a "paradigm shift," effectively creating a strategic model that could be transferred back to the same sectors that were used to build the model, and introduce innovative use of these same practices in new and different ways by corporations and nonprofit organizations.

A Strategic Triad

The Strategic Triad shown here illustrates the technological contributions of the Obama campaigns, and contrasts them with the current use of similar methods by organizations in other sectors of society (see figure 2.1). The three sectors represented include the political, corporate, and nonprofit sectors, and the technological innovations that were central to Obama's successful campaigns include social media, Big Data, and analytics and micro-targeting. There is an intriguing overlap across the three sectors, with some of the technological tools having been used for decades in one sector before their use in others, and some being used in new and different ways never even imagined only a few years ago.

The Obama presidential campaigns in 2008 and 2012 relied on business tactics and methods, just as earlier campaigns had done in the preceding sixty years. However, with their reliance on "state-of-the-art" marketing technology, the Obama campaigns "raised the bar" on many fronts, leading to the new paradigm shown in figure 2.1. No, this was not the first time the candidate, Barack Obama, had won office, as he accomplished that feat in 2006 when he was elected to the U.S. Senate. However, what was unique was the use of a combination of marketing tools that, when implemented in an integrative manner, made it impossible for any candidate to defeat him. This was also not the first time a candidate had run for the presidency using high-priced consultants – advertising gurus, marketing researchers, and a whole host of other specialists – who built an organization and a machine that was unstoppable once the momentum began to build.

It is now common knowledge among experts and citizens alike that both of the Obama campaigns used social media extensively to get his message out to younger voters who primarily relied on that communication vehicle for information about a wide range of products and services in the commercial marketplace. The pivotal use of social media on the part of the Obama campaign in 2008 brought out millions of new

Figure 2.1: A Strategic Triad

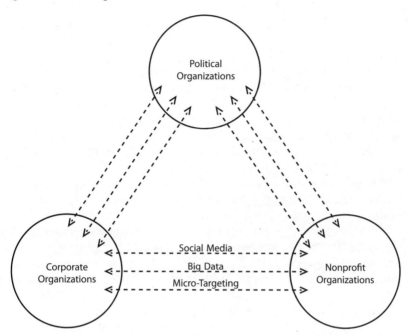

voters who had previously lost interest in politics.[5] Social media have become a staple in the strategic arsenal of most companies today, affording them the opportunity to use these technologies to spread the word about who they are via the Internet – from friend to friend and person to person – in a way never seen before.

Other innovative uses of technology in the Obama campaigns were so sophisticated and advanced, and so successful in achieving both victories, that they need to be analyzed in a new light. For example, one of the biggest success stories of the Obama campaign was the use of customer analytics.[6] The imperative of any marketing organization, including one centered on a candidate running for the presidency, must be to implement the marketing concept. All marketing organizations must understand the needs and wants of their customers, develop products and services on the basis of that orientation, and then frame and carry out a strategy with that in mind. The use of customer analytics by the Obama campaigns in 2008 and 2012 sets up the campaigns as case studies that can help us understand how technology can be integrated into the very fabric of a marketing organization. All marketing organizations succeed or fail on the basis of the correct understanding of their customer base, without which it becomes difficult to implement a winning strategy.

The Obama campaign teams treated analytics in a creative way never before seen in a presidential campaign. They realized that their competitors had data similar to theirs, so the big difference had to rest with the insights they could gain from the numbers and the effective use of that information to influence voters to support Obama. Voters who were most likely actually to vote for Obama were targeted very carefully. Constant testing of assumptions was always part of the strategic culture of each of the Obama organizations, especially the one developed for the 2012 campaign. Analytics were used not only to develop messages but also to solicit volunteers and money from donors.

The nonprofit sector is one of the most interesting areas where the use of similar technology illustrates a new and burgeoning role that organizations are playing in politics today.[7] Lobbying firms, interest groups, and other nonprofit organizations use the same marketing technology to raise funds, drive public opinion, and bring about victory for a particular candidate and/or political party. With spending limits now removed by the U.S. federal government and constraints lifted on how these organizations can use their money to support a political candidate, we are witnessing parallel campaigns for the presidency run simultaneously by both the political party and very wealthy donors who seek to put into power those politicians who support their pet causes. Going back in time, W. Clement Stone, a philanthropist who was a strong supporter of Richard Nixon, used his own money to help Nixon get elected. Today, there are numerous billionaires who are doing the same thing with a wide range of candidates. The shock here is not that it is happening but that the tactics that are being used are in some cases just as sophisticated technologically as those used by the politicians themselves.

The Obama Model

The Obama Model represents the latest manifestation of the evolution of marketing methods as they are used in politics. The 2008 campaign organization for Barack Obama began, as most do, with a meeting between the candidate and a group of people – a "kitchen cabinet," in the popular phrase – who started his process of running for the presidency several years before the election. In effect, it represented what is referred to in the business world as a start-up company. It had no roots other than as a team of people whose only goal was to win the White House. In 2012, the start-up organization that was brought together had the same mission as in 2008, but with a boost that capitalized on the brains trust used in 2008, along with the massive amount of information about voters from around the country that was generated from the use of the technologies identified in the Strategic Triad (see figure 2.1). At the heart of this whole process was a marketing organization that followed a standard set of steps that one would find in the marketing department of any corporation in the United States, or around the world for that matter. What is different, however, and what represented a new paradigm that can be followed by organizations in both the for-profit and nonprofit sectors, is the efficiency and effectiveness with which the Obama teams applied these tools.

In 2008, Obama, entered the race as an underdog, and in fact, outside the state of Illinois, was not very well recognized as a political leader in the country. This raises the question of how this relative unknown rose to become the leader of the free world. The answer lies in his use of marketing, relying on the creation of a movement that sought to put a president into the White House who represented all of the people, and who would bring an end to the war undertaken while George W. Bush was in office. Parallel with this movement came a wave of enthusiasm for this man reminiscent of the time when John F. Kennedy ran for the presidency in 1960. As both of the Obama campaigns unfolded, it would be his reliance on the technology transfers reported in the Strategic Triad that enabled his consultants to develop and test messages that resonated with segments of voters who were attracted to Obama for very different reasons.

In the 2012 campaign, Obama used experimentation to identify the correct words and passages to use in all forms of communication, whether through social media, e-mail, or any other media vehicle. The testing of the right words and phrases ensured that people would pay closer attention and respond in a positive way. Much of this process was initiated through the use of Big Data – again, a staple on the commercial side but put to use in innovative ways that trumped their uses by corporations before Obama's campaigns. The Obama strategists went beyond the use of data by Karl Rove, in the previous Bush campaigns, to analyze and determine exactly how many new voters were needed to win re-election for Bush. In 2008, Obama used Big Data to more carefully fine-tune the targeted communications that went out to different segments of voters. Along with the use of social media, this afforded the Obama team the ability to conduct a more "interactive" marketing campaign that ultimately allowed his staff to "turn on a dime" to respond to any competitive actions taken by his opponents. It was not a surprise to anyone who followed the career of Obama to know that as a community leader in Chicago he fine-tuned the art of reaching out to people; and he now extended this through the development of a large number of local offices that were set up all over the country. By relying on the World Wide Web as a fund-raising and organizing component in his campaign organization, Obama was able to generate record-breaking dollar donations in both of his campaigns.[8]

Another important part of the campaign strategy that sends a strong message to all marketers is that there are some fundamental axioms in politics that one cannot forget, and that other marketers need to know when to copy them and when not to. For example, money does not automatically mean you can buy a victory in the marketplace – or in an election. The campaign strategy also sends a message that changing demographics are not to be ignored, offline messages are still important, and, yes, television is still the dominant media vehicle. Enthusiasm still matters, as one only has to look at the difference between Obama's first and second debate performances in 2012, when he seemed to change from a boring, uninterested candidate in the first debate to a highly motivated, caring candidate in the second debate. For all marketers, the point here is that if you, the seller of the product or service, are not excited by and committed to what you produce, why should your customers be excited about what you sell? This is no different from Richard Branson's strategy when he constantly reminds his customers that he is more concerned that they have fun when they fly with Virgin Atlantic than he is with the details of airline travel. The Obama team used planning and flexibility to its advantage, too, another key part of any winning strategy.

An axiom that holds true in all marketplaces is the emotional connection that companies or candidates make with their customer base, donor rolls, or constituency, depending on the sector in question. One of the real success stories that came out of the 2008 campaign was the use of a movement to create a strong emotional response from many citizens in the United States who saw Obama as a political leader who would unite the many different factions in Washington, D.C. This was not the first time in U.S. political history that a movement had developed into a political campaign that was bigger than the candidate himself. Witness the campaign of Ross Perot, the plain-speaking politician who was able to take on the media in a way that no other presidential candidate had done prior to 1992. During the 1992 presidential campaign, Perot also introduced the political world to the "infomercial," a thirty-minute commercial that spent less time on splash and image and more on facts and figures, helping him to market himself as an authentic candidate of a type not seen before. The movement carried Perot pretty far, though not far enough to win the election.

The use of movements is not new to the world of business either, as Ralph Nader proved in the 1970s in taking on corporate America on many fronts. But the Obama movement in 2008 incorporated a different methodology that relied not only on technology and sheer boldness to position the candidate but on the use of marketing to create a machine of volunteers – many of them young college students – who supported and perpetuated the movement he started. The movement was just part of the emotional network that Obama used to his advantage.

Unlike a product or service, which may not elicit an emotional attachment, a political campaign at the presidential level relies heavily on the personality and charisma of a candidate to generate such an emotional attachment. The challenge is to use the technology that exists to translate emotion into electoral success. In this day of 24/7 coverage of every move a politician makes, especially if he is the leader of the free world, it is hard not to be seen daily by the American people. However, to take an example from previous presidential elections, such as the one in 1984 when Walter Mondale lost to Ronald Reagan, it was well known in political circles that Walter Mondale, when meeting people face to face, could connect with anyone on an emotional level. However, he seemed to stiffen up in front of a camera, and on television was never able to communicate with voters on an emotional level. That was not a problem for Barack Obama.

It is hard sometimes for a brand that does not easily evoke strong emotions to win over customers and motivate them to support and spread the word about a company and its products or services. Similarly, the use of negative emotions like fear to convince voters not to cast a ballot for a competing candidate, often used in politics (sometimes successfully), is less effective when it comes to trying to instill fear in Tide users, for example, and persuade them to switch to a competing brand. In politics, the attacks can take on a much more vicious tone; whereas with the selling of products the attacks are much more subtle, in part because of Federal Trade Commission laws designed to prevent a company from making exaggerated claims or leaving a false impression with consumers. Unfortunately, as a result of a 1971 Supreme Court ruling that equated political advertising with free speech, such laws do not exist in politics, making it easier for politicians to spread false rumors and even outright lies about competing candidates.[9]

The Obama strategists were careful not to spend more time than necessary on the competition. This is something that Obama was quite good at, always making references to his ideas for the future and spending less time on criticizing what his competitors were doing. In his second campaign in 2012, this is certainly not surprising, as he had a record, and along with that, the solid ground for Romney to attack him on. The position is similar for a corporation that has been in business for decades; its past may open it up to attack. The point is that people are always more interested in the positive than the negative. As part of the positive campaign message, Obama was not afraid to the let the public know what kind of family person he was. It helped Obama tremendously for the voters to know that he had a strong wife, who in some ways even pushed him around in the house. No, this did not create an image of Obama as a wimp; instead it depicted him as a sensitive partner who was in touch with his family's needs. It always helps to present a personal, human side to your customers.

A Blueprint for All Marketing Organizations

The Obama team was a marketing organization that created a consistent story that was connected with a compelling marketing message that each different audience they targeted could find relevant. Sound bites were based on a narrative that could be used over and over in slightly different ways, all of which were connected. For example, the infamous Clint Eastwood speech at the Republican Convention in 2012, where he had a conversation with an invisible Obama sitting next to him, was responded to on the Obama campaign website with the statement "This seat's taken ..." The phrase was the most popular tweet during the convention, but it was Obama's, not the Republicans'. Likewise, the Democrats' use of "Ask me anything" on Reddit set up a very popular two-way conversation with voters who sought to speak to celebrity endorsers. The point is that the big difference between 2008 and 2012 was that 2008 was the year of the first social media presidency, but 2012 was an evolution of the use of social media that went from focusing on community excellence to taking time to create excellence in content, making the marketing campaign consistent and meaningful, two of the most important attributes of any winning campaign.[10]

The real innovator on the political side of the equation when it came to raising funds over the Internet was Howard Dean, who, in his run for the 2004 Democratic presidential nomination, broke new ground by using this technology in a way it had not been used before, not even by Karl Rove in Bush's successful campaign in 2000. Similarly, one can look at the record amount of funds raised in Obama's two campaigns and point to the innovative use he made of the Internet. When it comes to raising funds – a necessary part of operating in the political market-place – nonprofit companies will definitely want to take a page out of the Obama playbook that successfully raised funds from millions of donors who were willing to contribute both small and large amounts of money. Every nonprofit seeks to understand better ways of generating funds for its organization, especially if it is not supported by the government or has no other external funding agencies to fall back on. Corporations, too, could benefit from the use of branding and advertising tactics identified as part of the Obama Model as they seek to maintain a unique brand identity and competitive edge in a crowded field of companies all vying for the loyalty of the same consumer segments.

The evolution of marketing in politics has reached a critical stage where politicians can no longer rely on a loyal party following but must be prepared to use any tool necessary to respond to unexpected events in a world that is changing every day. This challenge confronts all politicians and all governments, and is one that must be faced by any organization that seeks to be a leader in its respective marketplace. A variety of case studies from a range of industry sectors have been used to move the field of business forward for many years now. However, with the emphasis on the Obama Model, a blueprint emerges that represents the most up-to-date and innovative uses of marketing in a unique marketplace never before tackled. The Obama Model will be dissected in the next seven chapters, each of which describes a marketing lesson that will resonate with organizations targeting different markets but with similar challenges – challenges that were met in a creative and innovative manner by the Obama brains trust.

Chapter Two

Lesson 1: Follow the Marketing Concept

In all marketing campaigns, the imperative is to finely tune the marketing approach to focus on those customers or voters who will reward the efforts of an organization with the most bang for its buck. All historical references to best marketing practices always revert to a very basic theme, and that is to follow the marketing concept, which essentially states that all marketing decisions by an organization should be based on the dictum that the needs and wants of your customers must first be understood to help you determine which products and services to offer them. For the candidate running for office, that translates into a slightly more complicated set of offerings that will be explained later in this chapter. However, at the core of following the marketing concept is the strategic tool known as "micro-targeting."

Micro-targeting is a relatively new area in marketing that has its roots in the use of loyalty cards by retail stores to provide information to businesses about their customers. According to Cristina Ziliani and Silvia Bellini, micro-targeting provides new competitive tools, increases retail power, and encourages partnerships between companies and brands.[1] In a classic book that introduced this topic, Adam Brandenburger and Barry Nalebuff defined this process as one that enhances the competitive relationships within a distribution channel where the cooperation, conflict, and contractual aspects between supplier and retailer are concerned.[2]

A more recent publication suggests that market segmentation can be effectively achieved by grouping customers according to "combined transactional data of several customers and building a data mining model of customer behavior for each group." The point is that a micro-targeting approach is effective because it segments customers according to their comprehensive individual characteristics, not just their purchasing behavior. This approach goes beyond categorizing customers on the basis of statistical algorithms and instead brings together the transactional data of many different customers on the basis of their web-browsing activities.[3]

Micro-targeting involves the use of technological advances in database information acquisition, customer relationship management, relationship marketing, and a whole host of other very popular marketing tools, all of which emphasize the importance of delivering the right message to that segment of people who will be most likely to respond to your initiatives in a desired fashion. In simple terms, it means that the marketers of all products and services need to know who uses those products and services, why they use them, and whether or not they plan to use them in the future. Similarly, political organizations need to know who is committed to their candidate, who is not committed to their candidate, and who is leaning and susceptible to appeals that could move them to prefer their candidate if they currently don't. This is what following the marketing concept centers on, and micro-targeting is the strategic initiative that is used to implement this approach.

In a political marketing context, this same technology is used to shape political messages and their impact on the electorate. In fact, some experts in politics believe that micro-targeting in political campaigns reduces accountability on the part of politicians because it makes it difficult for the media to carry out research that accurately tracks messages tailored to specific audiences.[4] In the 2012 campaign, it became clear to all interested parties that Mitt Romney attracted a very different group of voters from those who preferred Barack Obama. As the campaign progressed through the primaries, into the conventions, and into the final stretch, it also became clear that each candidate's loyal followers were interested in different issues and policies being pursued by their respective leaders. Understanding what those issues and policies are is paramount to mounting a successful marketing campaign. However, once that information is determined, it is even more important that the implementation of the campaign's strategy is run as efficiently as possible to attract all possible voters, even those who may be what are referred to as "swing" voters, capable of leaning toward either candidate. The question then arises, what should the appeal be to each of these respective segments of voters? How should a message play out, in which medium, and with whom, as if it is being played out by actors on television? This is the fundamental challenge to marketers of politicians: to target the right message to the right people – in some cases, to one person at a time – through the appropriate channel.

Obama's strategists relied on a highly sophisticated micro-targeting campaign that allowed them to break down the marketplace of voters into segments that were likely to be influenced by particular advertising strategies. This called for the identification of the needs and wants of many different kinds of people – both voters and nonvoters. Perhaps the most innovative aspect was their use of secondary data on the lifestyles of different segments of voters to extrapolate and form predictions about their likelihood to vote for either Obama or Romney. Once that information was generated, the strategists were able to follow the marketing concept by establishing policies and supporting issues that tied into the lifestyles of these different groups of potential voters. So, what is new here? Both for-profit and nonprofit companies have been doing this for decades. What was new was the methodology the Obama team used to generate these data. In an effort that mirrors what all organizations try to do with their customers, the Obama team made each and every targeted voter feel as if he or she was a necessary part . of the equation.

The Evolution of the Marketing Concept

The development of the discipline of political marketing, along with technological changes in the ability to track the voter market, has created the ability to craft marketing strategies that are precise and accurate in their assessment of voter needs and wants. This has been well documented by many different political marketing experts, who have discussed in detail each of the major stages American presidential campaigns have gone through, from campaign organizations run by party bosses; to campaigns whose goal has been to find the best possible candidate to represent each of the two major political parties; to campaigns that centered on voters' reactions to the selling points put forward by the candidate representing each of the two parties; to organizations run by marketing experts whose goal is to identify voters' needs and wants and then develop political platforms to meet those needs.[5]

The evolution of the marketing concept represents a gradual shift in politics that has taken place over the past several decades in American politics.[6] Why the shift? It is clear that the movement toward a greater emphasis on marketing to drive political campaigns reflects significant structural and technological changes in society over the decades.

Structurally, the two major political parties have gradually lost power in the political process while other players have acquired more important roles, as is demonstrated by the increasing reliance on consultants and media strategists who understand the latest technological advances. Also, party affiliation as a predictor of future voter behavior has shifted as young people, less impressed with Washington insiders, have begun to pay attention to political candidates who are put forward not by a political party but by nonprofit organizations that reflect shifts in public opinion, such as the Tea Party, which was responsible for the shutdown of the U.S. government in late 2013.

This movement away from the political party redirected the focus of the political campaign organization away from party insiders who spend their careers working within a hierarchy with the hope of getting the nod from the party to represent their party as the nominee. A good example of this was Bob Dole, the Republican nominee in 1996. As a party insider, moving through the Senate and earning his "spot" on the ticket, Dole represented the "old" party orientation, running against Bill Clinton, someone who represented the strategic shift in politics toward candidates who may not have traditional career paths but are able to hire the best and brightest consultants to run their campaign. Certainly one would have to argue that the Clinton campaigns in 1992 and 1996 represented a big leap in marketing practice, especially the unorthodox use of a war room by Clinton's chief strategist, James Carville, who used the latest technological advances at the time to closely follow the marketing concept. Although the Bush campaigns that followed also relied on a marketing concept, it was not until the Obama campaigns that we witnessed another significant leap.[7]

Micro-targeting Is Critical to All Organizations

The effective use of micro-targeting by the Obama campaign in 2008 and 2012 has been well documented and explained in academia and the popular press (and will be outlined in detail later in this chapter), but its use by both for-profit and nonprofit marketers is not as widely studied. It has become abundantly clear from the Obama presidential races that the use of predictive analytics to aid in micro-targeting was essential to the success of his campaigns in informing voters and getting them to the polls on election day. However, how these same methods are applicable to business is not nearly as clear. The literature that exists tends to dwell on strategy and suggested uses of various marketing methods, with the topic of market segmentation still centered on segments of consumers as opposed to individuals. At the same time, there is evidence of micro-targeting based on our daily use of the Internet, as exemplified in banner ads based on search history, e-mail marketing based on purchases, and coupons that print at the point of sale at a supermarket. These in fact are all examples of highly targeted efforts to influence individual consumers based on company data.

It is possible that more attention is paid to this subject in politics than in commerce because of the higher level of urgency in politics, especially presidential politics, where a single purchase (or in this case a vote for a presidential candidate) is only made once every four years, without recourse for those buyers (or voters) who become unhappy with their decision. With all of this said, the use of micro-targeting as it exists today in for-profit organizations relies on analytics to narrow the focus of an organization and increase its marketing effectiveness and level of efficiency. For example, in multi-channel customer management, research suggests that some consumers use a company's website to find out about a product but wind up buying the product from another firm. There is also evidence of co-variates that could be used to predict this type of behavior, including income and education. The research in this area focuses on strategies to then convert the shopper who is just doing "comparison shopping" into a full-fledged paying customer. Research suggests that the most important issue in bringing about that conversion is the cooperative efforts within a company between website operations and the brick-and-mortar operation. In light of the current state of technological advances in commerce, it is recommended that organizations rely on the use of customer data to build up long-term relationships with individual customers.[8]

Following the Marketing Concept in the Clinton White House

In March 1995, I was brought into the West Wing of the White House to work with senior aides to President Clinton. At that first meeting, I met with Erskine Bowles (Deputy Chief of Staff); Don Bear (Director of Communications); and George Stephanopolous (Senior Aide to the President). The meeting centered on the issues surrounding the decline in popularity of President Clinton, and how those issues should be dealt with in an effort to develop a successful marketing strategy to get the president re-elected. After slightly more than two years in office, President Clinton found himself at the center of some embarrassing events that did not endear him to the American public. There was of course HaircutGate, when the president decided to get a $200 haircut on the tarmac of the airport in Los Angeles. That did not go over well with the image of a president who was still in the process of bringing the country back from a recent recession. There was also TravelGate, when Hillary decided to fire the entire staff of the travel department in the White House, another move that did not enhance the image of a president who appeared to be caught up in the minutiae of day-to-day activities in the West Wing.

Erskine Bowles, a venture capitalist, was brought in to bring order to a Clinton White House that seemed to be drifting and undisciplined, with a president who was famous for getting into conversations in the Oval Office and not spending enough time on matters that demanded his attention. With a new focus on discipline and time management came the realization in early 1995 that the President would need to do some rather spectacular things in a matter of months to get himself re-positioned to win office in 1996. This is where I and others, at different points in time, were brought into the West Wing to meet with senior staff members to try and figure out how to market Clinton (see the appendix, documenting correspondence with the Clinton White House). At our first meeting, I proposed a vision for the president that centered on the theme "The Restoration of the American Dream" as a way for him to win re-election in 1996. At the second meeting in the White House, on 8 February 1996, I presented to George Stephanopolous the results of a study carried out in October 1995. The study investigated how the President should reposition himself in the eyes of the American people via their perceptions of his ability to restore the American Dream. Throughout the course of the campaign to re-elect the president in 1996, Clinton spoke about building a bridge to the future, which implicitly made reference to the difficulties American citizens were experiencing and how he was going to make it possible for them to achieve the American Dream during his second term. From a marketing perspective, the challenge to the President was to define what the American Dream meant to different segments of voters and determine how best to incorporate those appeals in a promotional campaign.

During his re-election campaign, the President was able to convince voters that their struggles of today would lead to opportunity for their children tomorrow, and by so doing, he energized the electorate. He successfully appealed to voters on a multitude of levels, in essence implementing the use of the marketing concept and responding to people's needs and desires. On one level, he appealed to the "rational" side of citizens, offering them the financial stability to make their dream possible. On another level, he appealed to their sense of social equity in talking about opportunity for citizens from different backgrounds and countries and about giving each person an equal chance at achieving the American Dream. On an emotional level, he communicated a message that connected with people's fear of the current challenges they faced as well as their hope for the opportunities that would emerge in the coming years. Finally, he gave citizens something to look forward to, the hope of respite from their current constrained personal circumstances, by setting out changes he planned to make in his next administration that would pave the way for them to realize their own American Dream. In this way, Clinton relied on a marketing principle no different from Obama's in his two successful campaigns – connecting to people on an emotional, rational, social, and situational level through appeals targeting segments of voters. The big difference in the Obama model, of course, was extensive research based on the use of Big Data to carry out his marketing strategy over the Internet, a strategy that was not available in 1996 prior to the technological advances that had been made by 2008 and 2012.[9]

On a strategic level, I compared President Clinton, sitting as an unpopular president at our first meeting in March 1995, to a "defective product." I made the case for the importance of relying on a promotional strategy that would sell Clinton to the American people by having them look beyond his past failures and, at the same time, encourage them to connect with him on an emotional level. This strategy is one that I have always emphasized in all of my business consulting work, and I was convinced that, with the right theme, the President could do the same in the political marketplace. After carrying out several studies and conducting advanced multivariate statistical analysis, I determined that the American Dream (however that was defined, but for most people at the time it translated into owning a home, having a good job, living in a neighborhood free of crime, etc.) was dying for the American people, and what mattered most to citizens was the ability to make that dream a possibility for their children. In study after study, the same results came up, and I realized that this message would be one that could resonate with the American people, give the President an emotional link to the electorate (as everyone cares most about their families), and allow him to be marketed with an image that focused on future hopes rather than past failures.

Ultimately, in the 1996 election, the President's aides took my advice, slightly tweaking the results of my research and the themes I recommended to come up with their own version – as seen on 30 August 1996 in Chicago, when Bill Clinton promised to "build a bridge to the 21st century." The campaign was built around the essence of the strategy I had proposed, which was to offer hope to the American people (see the description in the appendix of the strategy given at the White House on 20 March 1995). This theme of hope was one that was slightly perplexing to me as a strategy when I asked at one of my meetings why the President simply did not use his own background as a poor boy from Arkansas who had lived the American Dream, a narrative that could be used as the centerpiece of his re-election campaign. Erskine Bowles astonished me when he responded that the President had a hard time talking about himself in public. I acknowledged that, and reiterated that the strategy I had proposed about making dreams come true for the young people of this country was paramount, and with it would come victory – which it did!

Following the Marketing Concept in the Bush White House

With the understanding that the political marketplace has progressed to the point where a political campaign is in fact a full-blown marketing campaign, always following the marketing concept, the question is: where did the process go after Clinton was re-elected? The answer lies in the successful campaigns of George W. Bush, who in 2000 and 2004 was elected and re-elected through the sage advice of Karl Rove. In part, Rove relied on the sophisticated use of a fund-raising machine that had been built up in the Republican Party over the previous decades, going back to the 1970s, when Richard Viguerie pioneered the political direct-mail industry and introduced his methods to presidential candidates, starting with Gerald Ford's run for the presidency in 1976. Republican fund raising benefited from Viguerie's methods in many subsequent campaigns, including those that were run by Karl Rove. Through careful crafting and clever maneuvering, Bush was marketed as the "anti-Clinton," a president who would restore integrity to the office that seemed to have been lost after Clinton was impeached. The strategy worked in 2000, and of course it is history now that the position in office put President Bush into the spotlight after 9/11 and cast him as a "war president" in 2004, an image that has worked for all recent presidents, except for his father, who lost in 1992.

To my surprise, at a meeting of Mexican politicians in Mexico City in 2005, shortly after Bush was re-elected, when I was sitting in the audience as one of several speakers, along with the keynote speaker, Matthew Dowd, Bush's campaign manager, Dowd spoke to the audience of 300 politicians about a Republican strategy that had never been reported in the news or made public in the United States. He revealed that the Bush strategy in 2004 revolved around an innovative calculation on the part of Karl Rove, who realized that Bush would be re-elected in 2004 if he was able to enlist 3 million new voters between 2000 and 2004. Relying on the connection of the Republicans with the evangelical movement in the United States, Dowd said that they went to the leaders of churches around the country and asked that they try to sign up at least ten new members to vote in 2004, and that the added 3 million votes would enable them to beat back the challenge of any candidate, even John Kerry. As it turned out, Bush beat Kerry by slightly over 3 million votes, with a 50.7 percent to 48.3 percent victory (62,040,610 compared to 59,028,444). Yes, one could argue that there were other factors as well, but the point is that the sophistication of political marketing moved to a new level during Bush's two terms in office, bringing into the equation a more careful analysis of voting patterns and an enhanced use of data.

The Use of Micro-targeting by Political Organizations

The goal of voter micro-targeting has been defined as the attempt to activate the base, persuade undecided voters, and improve partisan turnout. There is in fact a distinction that has been drawn in the field between narrowcasting versus broadcasting, which brings into the discussion another perspective on the use of micro-targeting in politics. In light of this distinction, the advantage of using micro-targeting is that it allows a campaign to allocate resources in the field very effectively, thereby creating new opportunities to get voters to go out and cast their ballot. So, the ultimate benefit of the use of this tool in politics is the ability to better predict the behavior of a voter.[10]

Ralph Reed, former Christian Coalition organizer, and founder of the Faith and Freedom Coalition, worked with Republican candidates with a micro-targeting strategy that sought to get out the evangelical vote in 2000. The strategy, as reported in *Time* magazine, was as follows:

> To identify religious voters most likely to vote Republican, the group used 171 data points. It acquired megachurch membership lists. It mined

public records for holders of hunting or boating licenses, and warranty surveys for people who answered yes to the question "Do you read the Bible?" … It drilled down further, looking for married voters with children, preferably owners of homes worth more than $100,000. Finally, names that overlapped at least a dozen or so data points were overlaid with voting records to yield a database with the addresses and, in many cases, e-mail addresses and cellphone numbers of the more than 17 million faith-centric registered voters – not just evangelical Protestants but also Mass-attending Catholics. One Republican consultant described this process as "backward micro targeting."[11]

This approach by Reed nevertheless leaves one somewhat unimpressed with where the Republicans are with respect to this new technology as compared to the Democrats during the two Obama campaigns. The gap in information centers on the use of procedures that only compare the profiles of people on multiple lists as opposed to "confirming" the target audiences you thought you understood. For example, Reed's micro-targeting system had the capacity to identify a woman who attended Mass and had a subscription to a Catholic charities newsletter, was married, with children, and living in a home worth more than $100,000; but it nevertheless wasn't designed to pick up another very important fact about this person – namely, that she regularly voted in Democratic primaries for federal and state offices. To have used this information to put her into a segment of voters thought to have been more predictive of voting for a Republican candidate would have been a huge mistake. In fact, for the person in question, it turned out that she was an Obama supporter.

This also raises the delicate issue that all targeting carries the risk of misclassifying voters whose attitudes are not consistent with their demographic and socio-economic profiles. "Outdated" thinking on the part of the Republican operatives left them "behind at the gate" as the 2012 campaign began. In fact, when it came to voter data and analytics, the two parties could not have been farther apart on the use of electioneering data in a modern campaign. This left the Obama team with a huge advantage when it came to polling, advertising, and fund raising, all of which were based on this micro-targeting technology.[12]

The technology used by the Obama team was first developed in the world of commerce, where companies that owned data warehouses – first created to generate credit ratings and then later used by direct-mail marketers – collected information on voters that, prior to recent presidential campaigns, had not been made available to political parties. The

Democrats worked feverishly to catch up with the Republicans after the Bush re-election in 2004, developing their own relationships with similar kinds of companies in the business of selling commercial databases and using that information to refine their own statistical algorithms. Ultimately, in politics, the main goal is to find out whose behavior will change in the future, and then determine the appropriate appeal to use to effect that change in behavior. The difficulty in politics is that the "customer" in question is not someone who uses either Brand X or Brand Y, but someone who may be leaning toward both brands, unsure which to go with. The challenge on the political side is to influence the behavior of those voters "on the fence" who aren't sure which candidate to vote for.[13]

The effectiveness of micro-targeting techniques in politics has been questioned by some as it becomes more difficult to ascertain the impact of these methods on campaigns because of the clandestine nature of politics, and the difficulty of being able to accurately measure isolated variables that come into play.[14] Others have argued that, while voters' views of candidates' platforms are far from complete, through the accumulation of social and consumer data, campaigns are able to discern which ideologies or platform issues will resonate and exploit that via targeted ads. Using this approach, candidates select a subset of issues, and voters use these selected appeals to align themselves to a candidate, creating the opportunity for a candidate to use a micro-targeting approach. At the same time, however, research indicates that electoral outcomes are not influenced by this technique and that the outcomes would not differ if the full electorate had full awareness of candidate platforms. As opposed to relying on micro-targeting, many campaigns are more centered on effectively promoting awareness of political issues and a candidate's platform.[15]

A Micro-targeting Model of Voter Behavior

If politicians and their strategists are going to follow the marketing concept and engage in the use of micro-targeting strategies, they need to identify models that enable them to break down the thinking of the voter into categories that can be easily translated into marketing appeals. One such model puts forward a set of five values that can be used to explain the behavior of a targeted audience of voters (see figure 3.1). The thesis of the model rests on the notion that a successful micro-targeting strategy should target likely voters and identify information about them that provides a basis for action. The model identifies five driving forces that shape a voter's behavior: *political issues, social imagery, candidate personality, situational contingency*, and *epistemic value*. The model itself has been tested in several elections and puts forward several cognitive beliefs that are derived from a wide range of sources. The fundamental message of the model is that voters are consumers of a service offered by a politician and, like consumers in the commercial marketplace, pick a candidate based on the perceived value the candidate offers them. The five values proposed represent different cognitive domains that drive the voter's behavior. One of the key propositions of the model is that a voter's behavior can be driven by a combination of one or more of the domains in a given election.[16]

The first value is the *political issues* component. This represents the policies a candidate advocates and promises to enact if elected to office. For a company, which this model is also applicable to, it refers to the appeals made to consumers that promise them benefits that have a rational appeal. The *social imagery* component represents the stereotyping of the candidate to appeal to voters by making associations between the candidate and selected groups of citizens in society. This use of imagery is very powerful as a way for the candidate to establish an association in the minds of voters between the candidate and selected supporters of the candidate. In the commercial marketplace, this is also operative, as companies are constantly seeking to create an image of their brand by establishing an association between the brand and celebrities in society.

Candidate personality represents the use of imagery in a slightly different way to emphasize a politician's personality traits in order to create an image for the politician. Similarly, in the commercial marketplace, marketers play on emotions all the time by using the right setting, appeals, and other factors to create a mood that influences a consumer's decision to buy a product. The *situational contingency* component represents that dimension of voters' thinking that could be influenced by an event that has either occurred or is expected to occur. On the commercial side, this serves to influence consumers who expect something to take place in an industry or a company that will drive them to alter their allegiance to the company. Finally, the *epistemic value* component represents the appeal to a citizen's desire for change and something new in a politician, just as consumers in the commercial marketplace are often looking for the latest brand or product. This micro-targeting model was used in the previously described work I carried out with the Clinton White House to reposition President Bill Clinton.

Figure 3.1: A Micro-targeting Model of Voter Behavior

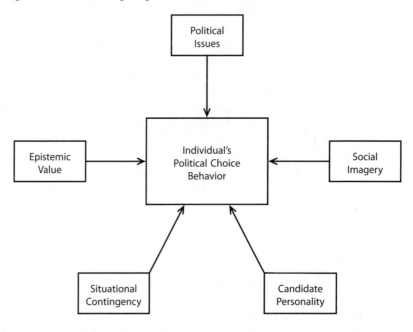

Application of the Micro-targeting Model to the 2012 Presidential Election

When we apply this model to the 2012 Obama campaign, it becomes clear that the use of each of the components to a greater or lesser degree proved to be critical in Obama's victory over Romney. The role of *political issues* was a centerpiece of the campaigns of both candidates, with Obama promising to continue on with his efforts to fix the economy and Romney making the point that Obama had not gone far enough in his efforts to eradicate the effects of the recession, and that Romney had the necessary leadership skills to bring about even more changes in the economy to reduce unemployment. As the campaign played out, Romney touted his skills as a successful executive who would take the same skills that had made him a very wealthy man and use them to create more job opportunities for the American people. In making this promise, Romney was leveraging the *candidate personality* component of the model to create a sharp contrast between himself and

Obama. The use of this component in the model was ultimately critical in Obama's victory over Romney, as the image of Romney as an out-of-touch multi-millionaire who did not understand the needs and wants of the American people prevailed in the advertising war that ensued. At the same time, Romney tried to use this same component to paint a picture of Obama as a failed leader who did not have the "right stuff" to continue to move the nation in the right direction.

This brings into play one of the most important strategic elements of the campaign, which was the effort to convince voters who were leaning in a particular direction to switch their votes to the opposing candidate, an element that ties in directly to the *situational contingency* component. There was a constant battle in the information and persuasion campaign of both organizations to move voters who were on the fence, not sure whom to vote for. The most effective tactical effort to carry this off relies on campaign appeals that promise everything to the voter and at the same time use excessive fear tactics to scare voters away from the opponent. The use of emotional appeals to create a sense of fear or some other strong feeling in voters is also very much part of the *candidate personality* component that relies on negative advertising to convey a message. Unfortunately, in politics today, though much less so in the commercial marketplace, negativity has become one of the most important tactical tools used by campaigns to influence voters vis-à-vis the *issues and policies* and the *personality* of their opponents.

Perhaps one of the most critical components that explains the use of the micro-targeting model is the *social imagery* component. The *social imagery* component establishes the image of a candidate through the association of that person with selected segments in the electorate. Both Obama and Romney used various approaches to "label" the other candidate through the use of the terms "liberal" and "conservative," both of which connote the connection of a politician to selected segments of the electorate. Along with this stereotyping, the terms "Democrat" and "Republican" also convey powerful messages about the attachment of groups in society to each of the candidates. One would have to conclude that Obama was more successful at labeling Romney a conservative only interested in benefiting the more financially successful people in society than Romney was at labeling Obama as an advocate for the "have-nots" and to some extent an a anti-business politician. These accusations and negative attacks in fact are often paid for by political action committees and interest groups who seek to curry favor with their constituencies to solicit more funds to carry out the attacks.

The last component yet to be discussed is the *epistemic value* component. In every presidential campaign, there is an effort to convince American voters that change is what each candidate will bring about if elected to office. American voters get tired of their leaders very quickly, and *epistemic value* certainly played a key role in 2012 when Obama had the difficult task of convincing voters that he in fact would deliver on his mantra from the 2008 campaign ("Change We Can Believe In") and would continue to make changes in government to deal with the challenges that lay ahead. This was not easy for the ultimate Washington insider, who had clearly leveraged that component in his first run for the presidency. He now had a record that voters could look at and use to evaluate him on, making it that much more difficult for him to use promises alone to curry favor with voters. Romney, on the other hand, was in a position to use this component to leverage his own position, as the only record he had to run on was his role as governor of Massachusetts. However, with the summer before the election leaving Romney without much money in his campaign coffers because of a bruising primary fight with his opponents, the Obama campaign went on a spending binge and used millions of dollars in advertising to label Romney as a "rich" person who was out of touch with the average American, and much too risky a candidate for voters to put in the White House. The gamble on the part of the Obama campaign worked, and Romney was never able to shake the image or convince voters he was an agent of change.

As one considers each of these components as part of a micro-targeting effort, it is important to take note of the fact that the key to marketing during a presidential campaign is ultimately to understand the needs and wants of the voters. The strength of this model lies with the infinite variety of appeals that can be generated from its use, and the knowledge that every voter during a presidential campaign decides to cast a ballot for one or another candidate on the basis of many different reasons, each of which is spelled out in this model. Let's now take a look at each of the two Obama campaigns and point out the tactical maneuvers that were used to follow the marketing concept.

The Obama Model

Obama's campaign director in 2008, David Plouffe, made the point that the goal of the campaign was not only to ensure high participation and turnout of their base but to expand the size of the electorate by mobilizing first-time voters, mainly among young adults and minorities. This is a familiar strategy on the commercial side, where companies often seek to attract nonusers to try their product at least once in an effort to create a brand-loyal customer. On the political side, it becomes a more challenging task to motivate a citizen, first to go out and vote, and second to cast a ballot for a particular candidate. In an effort to reach out to these citizens, Plouffe focused on the Internet and text message strategies, sending out more than 1 billion e-mails over the course of the campaign, and effectively turning the website (then called my .barackobama.com) into a key strategic weapon during the campaign.[17]

For the 2012 campaign, this methodology was then enhanced by the Obama team, beginning when Jim Messina arrived in Chicago as Obama's new campaign manager in January 2011. Messina had a hard and fast rule for all recruits into the campaign: All decisions were to be based on measurable data. In 2008, the campaign was data driven, but in 2012, under Messina's leadership, this thinking was extended even further.[18]

As they began their strategic efforts for the second campaign, the Obama team recognized that demographic shifts had permanently changed the landscape of America. In 2011, for the first time in U.S. history, nonwhite babies outnumbered white babies. Although many corporations have "diversity marketing" groups, the question arises just how closely marketing managers are paying attention to the different needs and wants of these communities. What the Obama team realized early on is that all marketing is local. Based on Messina's experience as an organizer in Chicago, he knew that organizing was essential to a successful operation, and he opened up over 700 field offices as compared to only 300 for Romney. The point here is that each of these offices had a better understanding of the local needs and wants of their constituents than the people at the center of the operation working out of D.C. (This sends a strong message to all organizations, both for-profit and nonprofit, about the importance of giving more control to local executives running their operations around the world.[19])

Sasha Issenberg used the same kind of data that were used by the Obama campaign to develop his own poll, which many believed to be one of the best during the 2012 campaign cycle. Issenberg made a strong case for the argument that politicians had moved ahead of corporations in their use of Big Data, not only in identifying key issues of concern to voters and making accurate predictions on that basis but also in using the data to actually change people's behavior. According to Issenberg, the Obama campaign team not only knew who voters were but were able to turn voters into the type of citizen they wanted them to be. He believed that the campaign had as many as 1,000 variables of information on each voter, obtained from voter registration records, consumer data warehouses, and prior campaign contacts made with the voter. In 2012, this use of "data mining" was based on public and private databases some of which dated back as much as two decades.[20]

Issenberg stressed that a large part of the success of their use of micro-targeting in 2012 was the ability to use the data to predict which advertising campaigns would be successful. Obama wound up hiring Carol Davidsen, who had previously worked with organizations where other data sets were held in TV Internet boxes. Davidsen was able to negotiate with research firms that aggregated this data for other clients and have them repackage it in a form that could allow the Obama campaign access to individual histories without violating existing privacy standards. By then matching this data with Obama team databases of persuadable voters and their addresses with cable billing fields, the team was able to create its own television ratings system in an effort to make optimal media choices. Joe Trippi, Howard Dean's consultant in 2002, had pushed for a "bottom up" as opposed to a "top down" approach to the use of technology to form a strategy that was centered on the needs, desires, and aspirations of voters – the core of micro-targeting. This led to many innovations, one of which was Obama's ability to raise $500 million online from over 13 million people who had signed up for his campaign by 2007. This also allowed Obama's 2012 team to build a national campaign on the back of Big Data. Unfortunately for Hillary Clinton in 2008, and Mitt Romney in 2012, both relied on a "top down" approach, and both lost. The net effect was to work against the logic of a grassroots organization pushing strategy.[21]

In the 2012 campaign, more than $10 billion was spent on the campaign by all candidates. The online portion of that was approximately $160 million, eight times more than the $20 million spent in 2008. Some of the key findings of a report on this phenomenon suggest that political messages that are delivered online fit the model that relies on this logic. In other words, it is possible through online technology to target individuals with specific messages geared to their preferences and likes and dislikes in a candidate that connect with that candidate's policies.[22]

During the 2012 campaign cycle, micro-targeting was done by many different members of political campaign organizations, including consultants, public relations advisors, and media advisors. As the world of politics continues to follow the marketing concept, there is an attempt by all parties to reach "niche" voters and groups who must be communicated with on a customized basis. The conclusions of many experts is that 2012 was the year that online political advertising matured in the way television advertising matured in the 1960s, when the Johnson campaign's famous Daisy commercial demonstrated the power of advertising to influence the electorate. Although advertising on the Internet has been omnipresent since the 1990s, the Howard Dean campaign in 2004 and the Obama campaign in 2008 represented critical shifts in this paradigm and took it to new levels of sophistication.[23]

In the 2008 and 2012 campaigns, Big Data brokers, including Acxiom, Experian, and others, partnered with the Obama campaign, and after removing information that identified specific individuals, which they were required to do by law, they were able to collate the information and, following a marketing concept, target messages to citizens by either e-mail, direct mail, or social media, depending on which outlet best fitted the purpose of the message, be it a request for funds or volunteer help or simply a message about a particular Obama policy. The process was very much influenced by a 2010 Supreme Court ruling, *Citizens United versus FEC*, which, for the first time since 1907, permitted unlimited spending on political advertising by corporations and unions. This opened up the floodgates for money to pour into the system, providing a financial foundation for these activities. Before this ruling, only the candidates themselves could advertise for or against a politician running for office, and outside groups were limited to advertising that did not support a candidate. The spending free-for-all was further fueled in 2012 when, for the first time in a presidential election, both major candidates opted out of using taxpayer funding for the general election, thereby avoiding restrictions on the amount of money they could spend. As early as June 2012, fund raising by both candidates and their supporters had exceeded $1 billion, and approached $10 billion for all contests.[24]

One of the great contributions from the Obama campaigns was their fine-tuning of the ability to follow and understand the needs, wants, and aspirations of potential voters whom they thought they might be able to influence. Part of this effort stemmed from the desire on the part of the Obama team to win back voters who had taken themselves off the campaign's e-mail list. Specifically, those who had been on the list in 2008 but had removed themselves from the list for the 2012 campaign were key targets. In one very effective tactic, micro-targeting was used during the campaign to set up a series of dinners with Obama that were generously hosted by celebrities, including actor George Clooney and other film stars. This proved to be a very successful marketing campaign. Using a demographic database, the offer was sent out to selected citizens, with the understanding that they would have dinner with a celebrity and Obama if they won. It turned out that West Coast women aged forty to forty-nine were the most likely to make a contribution to have a chance at dinner with Clooney and Obama. Other popular celebrity hosts included *Sex and the City* star Sarah Jessica Parker, *Vogue* editor Anna Wintour, and singer-songwriter Mariah Carey. Interestingly enough, the demographic group that proved to be most interested in those dinners was also the West Coast woman aged forty to forty-nine.[25]

There were some material differences in the application of micro-targeting techniques between the two Obama campaigns. Although micro-targeting was a relatively new concept in 2004, by 2008 it had become integral to every aspect of the Obama campaign, from the caucuses to the general election. In 2012, there was an even bigger difference with respect to working with online data. On the Republican side, Romney used much more sophisticated micro-targeting tactics than McCain had in 2008. (The big challenge in 2012 in reaching voters was the ability of citizens to use call-forwarding, caller ID, and privacy managers to avoid telephone calls from political canvassers.) With the advances made in the 2012 campaign, it became possible to use online space in real time, meaning it might take only a few days as opposed to a few weeks to get information back from a survey and analyze the data to build a database of prospective voters. Ultimately, the database was used to create "scores" attached to voters that identified them as either more or less likely to be open to influence. It should be noted, however, that while the speed of obtaining useful information improved greatly from 2008 to 2012, the explanatory power of the models still leaves room for improvement.[26]

Following the Marketing Concept to Better Understand Consumers

Looking back at the mid-1980s, we can see that there was much potential for the introduction of new technology to allow us better insight into the thinking of consumers, but that the analytics were not there to support its use. The general direction of this field was clear at the outset, which was that measuring and tracking both all sales records of even the most minimal amounts of money and the usage metrics of any interest to a company would result in a better understanding of all relationships with those doing business with the company. The net result of that orientation is that today huge databases touching every dimension of the world we live in are available at the click of a computer mouse. However, there are some problems associated with this paradigm shift.[27] General Motors, a company known for innovation in the automobile industry, can be congratulated as also being very innovative as a marketer. In an effort to help its salespeople understand how to respond to customer needs better, in 2012 GM used the Disney magic and sent 2,300 of its Chevrolet dealers and 600 of its Chevrolet division employees to three-day Disney Institute training sessions in Orlando, Florida, and Anaheim, California, to introduce them to the "living laboratory" that typifies the Disney experience for their customers. It turns out that Disney managers get a 70 percent retention rate, meaning that 70 percent of their customers return to their parks, a very high loyalty rate. This is clearly an example of a company that is working hard at following the marketing concept, encouraging its employees to respond to customer needs by initiating dialogue with them instead of letting them sit in a parking lot waiting to enter the dealership to look at cars.[28]

In a partnership between IBM and Toshiba, analytics tools were used to get a better understanding of some of Toshiba's customers. IBM worked with Toshiba to create a new technological system called TCxGravity. This application allowed IBM to link order management technologically to provide a multi-channel view of a customer's purchase history at the checkout. This allows retailers, for example, to carry out personalized activities like making a targeted offer to a customer based on previous purchases, as well as to make recommendations to a customer on the basis of their purchase history for items that are out of stock. In effect, this micro-targeting effort, following the marketing concept, introduced "real time" decision-making capabilities. Combining this information with a positive customer interaction allows the retailer to target product recommendations. This "customer-centric" trend – toward sales and marketing built around customers' needs and wants – is one area that IBM is working to build up within the company.[29]

Google is another example of a company using this same technology in a slightly different way. Google is using technology to make its advertisements more relevant and personalized by targeting advertisements to customers whose needs match a company's offerings. For example, Google ads are developed in a "real time" format that matches the interests of a person online at a specific moment in time. So, if someone is searching for a stereo on Google, ads will automatically pop up that tie into that product category.[30]

Going a step further, some companies are looking at people's habits to make a determination of their future purchase patterns. In a slight twist to this application, but relying on the same principles, Tony Dungy, former football coach for the Indianapolis Colts from 2002 to 2008, propelled one of the worst teams in the NFL into stardom by focusing on how his players reacted to field cues during a game in a habitual manner, helping to bring out the best in his players. Ann Graybiel, an MIT neuroscientist, reported on how her colleagues began to explore habits several years ago by putting their wired rats into a T-shaped maze with chocolate at one end. The maze was structured so that each animal was positioned behind a barrier that opened after a loud click. The first time a rat was put into the maze, it would walk very slowly up and down the center aisle after the barrier slid away, sniffing in corners and scratching at walls. It appeared that the rats were able to smell the chocolate but could not figure out how to find it. It seemed as if there was no discernible pattern in the movements of the rats, but probes that were connected to their brains told a very different story. What the researchers eventually learned was that as the rats learned how to complete the maze more quickly, the mental activity decreased. As the path became more and more automatic, and it became a habit, the rats began to think less and less, and only act.[31]

When one extrapolates this thinking to voters – or consumers, for that matter – the creation of habit must be understood from an explanatory point of view, not just a predictive point of view. There needs to be a conceptual framework that allows marketers of any kind of product, service, or idea to go from an understanding of the cognitive makeup of a decision maker to a predictive model that can be reinforced in the future with this understanding of how habits are formed.

The process by which the brain converts a sequence of actions into an automatic routine is what is referred to as "chunking." We all go through such chunking patterns hundreds of times daily. Some may be as simple as opening up a can of beans before pouring them into a pan; others are more complicated, like putting together a dinner for a family of four. Still other even more complicated chunking procedures, like a behavioral response to a wife or husband on a daily basis, can also be understood with this kind of modeling. In fact, many people may be quite surprised to realize that they are engaged in such activities on a daily basis.[32]

This understanding can be used to capitalize on people's e-mail behavior patterns – for example, what they do when a computer or mobile device chimes, alerting them that a new e-mail has just arrived. This insight was an integral part of the Obama team's effort at micro-targeting citizens. Let's say that the Obama camp sends out an e-mail to a list of citizens. After the computer chimes with the new message, the recipient's brain starts to anticipate the neurological pleasure associated with clicking on the new e-mail and reading the message. These same expectations that a person has throughout the day can build up until the person is moved to the point of distraction by the thought of an e-mail sitting there unread on his or her computer. If, on the other hand, the alert is removed from the computer or cell phone, the craving to get the information is never triggered.

In corporate America, Procter & Gamble used this "chunking" concept in their marketing to turn a product that was failing into one of its best sellers. In the mid-1990s, the company started a secret project to create a new product that could eliminate bad odors. They spent millions on a colorless, cheap liquid that could be sprayed on a couch that smelled, or a shirt that stank, to make the odor disappear. The product is called Febreze. To market the product, the company formed a team that included a former Wall Street mathematician, Drake Stimson, along with habit specialists, whose job was to make sure the television commercials accentuated the cues and rewards of the people shown using the product. One of the first commercials showed a woman complaining about the smoking section of a restaurant. She complained that whenever she ate at the restaurant, she found that her jacket smelled like smoke when she got home. In a similar commercial, a woman was shown worrying that when her dog sat on the couch with her, it left a bad odor on the couch. She was then shown with a friend saying that her furniture would smell better if she used Febreze. Unfortunately for the company, the ads did not work at first. So Procter & Gamble hired a Harvard professor who was asked to look at the ads. After collecting hours of footage of people watching the ad, they went into the field and visited a woman who said her house was not perfect, but she always used Febreze. When she was asked for which odors she used the product, she said it was not used for specific smells but for a normal cleaning of the house. She said after she used a couple of sprays in the room, she felt like it was a mini-celebration after she finished. It turned out to be a winning advertisement for the company.

Using the Marketing Concept to Better Understand Donors

In the nonprofit world, the website has become the communication hub between an organization and its members, just as it has in the for-profit world. This means that a nonprofit website must be fully developed, with the organization's mission and cause and activities built into it. The website has to be constantly updated with new events that take place, tweets from appropriate people, and visuals to give visitors a very positive image of what the organization represents.[33]

Charitable organizations are an example of nonprofit companies that use this new technology to implement a marketing concept. One such organization is Cornerstone Restoration Ranch, which relies on micro-targeting to help people in need. The ranch provides food, housing, and faith-based rehabilitation services for troubled members of the San Diego community. The founder, Cheri Colt, made the point that, "unlike most rehabs I have encountered, we teach our participants to live beyond the initial six months of getting to learn the power of Christ to give their members the tools they need to truly enrich their lives and get onto prosperous paths." They use natural surroundings to set the stage. Working with an Internet company, Rocketforce.net, they were able to make their web presence more effective, as it was in a state of much-needed repair. (Rocketforce.net is a full-service Internet marketing and web development company whose mission is to integrate a micro-targeting orientation into nonprofit organizations.[34]) The company helped the nonprofit build a custom website that was able to facilitate the donations that were coming in.

Another good example of a nonprofit company that has implemented such a strategy is the United Way. They launched a social campaign aimed at helping inner-city people in Milwaukee. Partnering with a services marketing firm to launch their online campaign, they used Facebook videos to address issues such as teen pregnancy and statutory rape, and to promote strategies for building healthy relationships with other people. In October 2010, the general understanding in the community was that limited Internet service among the African-American population in the inner city could reduce the effectiveness of social media campaigns. Although most inner city homes did not have Internet connections, their residents nevertheless had put a large number of Facebook pages online. However, the need to connect with their peers still existed. So United Way kicked off a campaign at a Milwaukee Fatherhood Summit, where more than 200 men recorded their videos on Facebook. The goal was to target the audience for the campaign with the wisdom of men they knew, were in interested in talking to, and knew they could relate to. The participants attempted to reach more than 100,000 of their peers with videos and messages addressing a variety of topics, including the negative effects of older men spending time with younger girls; the link between statutory rape and teen pregnancy; the fears of a young father; how to respect a woman; and important things men want their children to know about building healthy relationships. The campaign included a contest for the best video based on voting online, and the winner received an Apple iPad. It was a great success.[35]

The Importance of the Relationship When Following the Marketing Concept

While all businesses would agree that they would not exist without their customers, many lose sight of the importance of that relationship. The word "relationship" of course implies that there exists an effective mechanism customers can use to contact a firm to have their needs better met or their concerns addressed. In some cases, simple issues – where a customer states that a product or offering failed to meet his or her expectations – can escalate into a nationwide story highlighting incompetence and bureaucratic red-tape.

For example, take the case of Dave Carroll, a singer-songwriter traveling with his band for a show in Nebraska who was alerted by another passenger that the baggage handlers were throwing guitar cases during a transfer at Chicago's O'Hare airport. Carroll, knowing that the guitars were most likely those of the band, spoke with three United Airlines employees about the mishandling and was "met with indifference." Upon inspecting his luggage at the end of his trip he discovered that his guitar neck had been broken. After he had spent a year trying to resolve the issue through e-mails, phone calls, and talking to supervisors at higher and higher levels, his claim was denied. During the year, Carroll offered many solutions. Carroll originally asked that the airline pay to replace the guitar, then that the airline simply reimburse him for the cost of repairs; eventually he even offered to accept the replacement value ($1,200) in flight vouchers. United refused all of Carroll's proposed solutions, citing guidelines, or red tape, or some way in which he had neglected to follow correct claim procedures. Once his report was denied, Carroll took matters into his own hands. He wrote and performed a song titled "United Breaks Guitars" and posted it on YouTube where it became a viral sensation. The video, which eventually sparked songs and parodies and innumerable articles in various publications, resulted in millions of negative impressions seen around the world. By 2011 the original video had had more than 14 million views, and Carroll's experience is now used as a case study in business schools around the country. When the video reached 150,000 views, United offered to pay Carroll to take the video down. In effect, saving $1,200 cost United millions of mentions of their poor customer service.[36] This example of how customer relationships can be broken also provides a roadmap of best practices in cultivating and maintaining positive relationships that bring value to customers and firms alike.

Technology Is Driving the Marketing Concept

Over the past decade political campaigns, interest groups, and a wide network of private companies have developed highly sophisticated tools to better understand how very small numbers of the electorate think, live, and behave. For example, campaigns have access to the voting histories, housing values, recreational preferences, automobile ownership, and television and Internet viewing habits of potential voters. This has happened alongside the rise in information about consumers revealed through credit card usage and Nielsen ratings – information that has become a tool used in recent campaigns around the country. As well, the past decade has seen advances in the speed of computers and more sophisticated software that have stimulated a new political industry that uses nano-targeting and micro-targeting to reach voters with messages that will resonate with them. In 2004, the Bush campaign, thought by many to be a pioneer in the use of micro-targeting, used an anti-gay message sent to socially conservative black voters in the key battleground state of Ohio, resulting in a change from 9 percent support from this segment in 2000 to 16 percent support in 2004. Along with this came a decrease in support for the Democratic candidate, from 89 percent support for Gore in 2000 to 84 percent support for Kerry in 2004. In broader terms, this strategy has helped to fuel the polarization of the country, as campaigns use this kind of information to emphasize issues that will either broaden or suppress turnout among a segment of voters.[37]

The election campaign of Barack Obama in 2012 offered the world a glimpse of where politics is headed. In the final days of the campaign, as some pollsters were forecasting a very close outcome, experts in the Obama camp were making use of Big Data, deciding with precise accuracy which voters were the key to victory and how to get those people to vote on election day. This is a far cry from the days previous to this in the business world, where companies would target customers on the basis of demographic and lifestyle characteristics. Marketers, with the knowledge of the success of the Obama team, can now target potential customers with greater precision because of the greater number of "touch points" (meaning opportunities to make contact with their customers). The real challenge is to figure out how to make the right offer, to the right customer, at the right touch point, at the right time. This is not to say that the fundamentals of marketing – the importance of following the marketing concept, building a strong brand, making people aware of it, and earning their loyalty so they become repeat purchasers – have changed in any way.[38]

Companies today are using advertising agencies to implement the new online strategies, and at the same time are trying to make decisions that involve investing large amounts of money in the "right" promotional campaign. Decisions may involve the choice between putting millions of dollars into a sixty-second commercial during the Super Bowl or using that same money to mine more data. The danger here is that technical people who are making these decisions may not be in a position to fully understand the marketing implications driving the growth of a company. Someone who has knowledge of digital marketing and social media may not understand marketing in general. The Obama team was able to achieve victory through integrating the activities of people working out of the same office – in some cases, the same cubicle. In a start-up company or a political campaign people are forced to sit at the same table, but this kind of integration may not be as easy to achieve in a company with a more traditional structure.[39] For-profit and nonprofit companies need to be careful to ensure that the people using these advanced techniques work together in an integrated manner. This topic is discussed in more detail in later chapters.

Chapter Three

Lesson 2: Use Technology Strategically

Over the past several decades, technology has found its way into all facets of political campaigns, from the amassing of databases, to the creation of advertising appeals and political commercials, to fund raising, to volunteer network development, and to the communication with a whole host of publics, all of whom have a role in the political process. The technological advances have all gravitated from the business world to the political world, in tandem with a reliance on consultants and experts who have been able to make the leap in logic from products and services to politicians, political parties, and even the running of government.

As technological advances have been made in politics, the groundwork has been laid for marketers to carry on a conversation between different groups of people, each of whom may have a vested interest in the outcome of the election results. The conversation that was carried on throughout both of Obama's successful presidential campaigns relied on a use of technology that allowed the campaign to create links online in different websites to make the conversation real for those following it.[1]

Technology in Politics

The same campaign consultants who were responsible for putting Barack Obama into office in 2012 were hard at work doing the same for other Democratic candidates running in off-year elections. Democratic candidate Terry McAuliffe hired the service of BlueLabs, a company that worked with the Obama team in 2012. By going through reams of data, the company worked to identify whom to target with their advertising and grassroots efforts, as well as which appeals to use. After identifying some issues that McAuliffe advocated that appealed to Republican voters, the consulting team quickly pushed the campaign to expand their voter turnout efforts in different parts of the state, places where Democrats don't normally do well. One of the experts who worked with the Obama team in 2012, Dan Wagner, started his own consultancy firm, Civis Analytics, in early 2013. It didn't hurt that he had the financial backing of former Google Inc. CEO Eric Schmidt. Another of Obama's gurus who ran the campaign's media operations, Larry Grisolano, started his own company, Analytics Media Group, to help candidates buy television ads, using analytics to make low-cost buys on niche and late-night programs that would reach persuadable voters.

For many years now, organizations in the commercial sector have been building profiles of their customers in an effort to target them with advertising appeals that resonate with their needs and wants. Techniques used over the years have included customer surveys and secondary sources of consumer data that reveal consumers' buying habits, media usage, lifestyle patterns, and other characteristics that highlight differences between market segments. The Obama team moved this paradigm forward significantly through micro-targeting methods and customer analytics that used data-mining techniques to analyze very large databases of telephone interviews and test messages with voters, making as many as 11,000 telephone calls per night in the top battleground states. Strategists were able to use data to determine all facets of strategy, including where to target direct mail, e-mail, and other voter contacts, and what messages to use. According to BlueLabs, their job was to "figure out, through the modeling process, who the people are who are going to be most receptive to that idea," and not to write the script for the candidate. The challenge to the consultants for hire was to repeat the success of the Obama campaign effort.[2]

One of the great lessons from both Obama campaigns was in the use of analytics as a creative force that allowed them to keep tweaking ideas until they were perfected, a strategy that required the team to keep testing the marketplace on a regular basis. The imperative here was for the Obama team to focus on those citizens who had the greatest likelihood of being affected by their efforts – the swing voters who hadn't made up their minds yet. Naturally, as in any campaign, the most "persuadable" voters are always the ones a campaign wants to target. The challenge is to identify exactly who they are.

Big Data and Analytics Are Driving Marketing Decisions

In organizations across the country, large amounts of information that would once have been unmanageable can now be tracked and stored for further analysis. Many companies are in fact creating entire departments with employees who have expertise in analytics and Big Data. Advances in this area allow organizations to learn from the behavior patterns of their current customers, and then respond with tactical solutions that allow them to provide customers with desired benefits in an effort to maximize their profits.[3] Even though organizations are translating big databases into information that allows them to respond to their customers in a more efficient manner, there still exists a talent gap that enables organizations to optimally leverage the use of all of this information. This is due in part to the attitudes that organizations have toward the use of this type of technology.[4]

In a study carried out on 325 data management professionals, findings suggest that there are several trends in the industry. One key trend, when the economy is not doing well, is that companies look for more efficient ways to spend their money.[5] A report by McKinsey Consulting examined the use of technology to improve performance for employees and executives. Their findings suggest that it is critical to use the right data and to integrate analytics into the day-to-day operations of a firm. They point out that alternative sources of data are available, and organizations must be sure that their information technology platforms are able to leverage the use of various databases. They conclude by saying that this kind of technology should be used to develop predictive models of behavior, and that it can be very risky for organizations to overhaul their overall business on the basis of findings from analytics on a trial-and-error basis.[6]

When it comes to the use of databases, all organizations need to realize that the analysis of this information can lead a company down several different roads. Furthermore, data are no substitute for an understanding of how and why consumers respond emotionally in the marketplace, and this needs to be considered when a marketing manager reviews the results of data crunching. In other words, while data analysis may indicate why certain products and services have excelled in the past for an organization, it cannot replace the judgment of an executive who understands the whims of his or her core customers and can gauge the likelihood that an innovative product will succeed when there are no data on which to base that prediction.[7]

What Is "Big Data"?

In one of the most cited works in this area by the McKinsey Global Institute (MGI), the authors point out how companies navigate the vast pools of data and identify the various domains that Big Data has transformed (health care, public sector, retail, manufacturing, and personal data). They also discuss the implications for policy makers and business leaders. According to the authors, Big Data creates transparency, helps discover new possibilities and improve performance, facilitates effective segmentation, supports human decisions with groundbreaking algorithms, creates new business models, and helps industries innovate. The study provides a comprehensive set of knowledge and practical applications from one of the most reputable consulting companies in the world.[8]

In some critical reviews of Big Data, scholars argue that there is a great deal of confusion about the meaning of the term, and that it has less to do with the size of the data pool than with the ability to aggregate and cross-reference data sets. Also, the quality of data is more important than the size of the data pool. It is argued that the sample of a data set is crucial to establish the relevance of the data. Furthermore, they note that "Big Data" refers not only to large data sets but also to the procedures used to manipulate information, and to the ethical issues raised by the use of this technology.[9]

There is no doubt that the advances made in data mining and analytics, as well as the ability to access huge databases as the result of increases in storage capacity, have given information scientists in all fields an unprecedented capability to obtain information and use it in both business and government. The use of data to increase the productivity of companies and allow them to innovate on a larger scale is creating opportunities that also raise serious privacy issues. There is the distinct possibility of a backlash both from government and from regulatory agencies that seek to protect individuals in society.

Although the terms "Big Data" and "analytics" are often referred to in the same context, there are important distinctions between them. In fact, "analytics" echoes the term "consumer analytics" commonly used by company marketing managers to refer to the technology used by marketing experts to analyze data about the behavior patterns of current customers. For example, consumer analytics technology allows airlines to alter airfare prices based on the day of week, in an effort to maximize profits.[10] With this in mind, it is suggested that whereas data gathering is being continually improved, the development of "actionable metrics" is also needed to leverage this kind of technology, and that currently there is limited know-how about how to carry out the task. This has led business schools around the United States to work feverishly to develop new programs, majors, and certificate programs to train professionals with the needed skills. Part of the problem here has to do with the accelerating pace of change, as data-oriented executives seek to respond to an increasingly fluid environment while facing resistance from those with more traditional mindsets in their organizations. In a study carried out on more than 300 data management professionals, the conclusions drawn suggest that a good base to move from in organizations centers on a compilation of best practices within industries that put forward solutions to make more efficient uses of marketing dollars.[11]

In another report on this technology change, the authors sought to focus on the most effective uses for big data and customer analytics. A report developed by McKinsey Consulting looked at the design of analytics programs and how they are being used by both employees and executives. The report offered conclusions on how to integrate analytics into the daily operations of an organization. Among their findings, the authors suggest that it is critical that the "right data" are used, and that the data should match the information technology infrastructure within the organization. The authors also suggest that it is risky to attempt to completely overhaul the core business on the basis of analytics findings, a course that may put the company in a "short-term-solution" mode that could result in negative outcomes. Instead they suggest a three-step process to use analytics successfully to bring about change: beginning with the use of multiple data sources; focusing on optimization models – meaning they should strike a balance between the ease of use and the complexity of the models; and finally, creating simple, easy-to-understand tools for employees on the front lines. They predict that the United States in fact may face a shortage of as many as 140,000 to 190,000 people with the appropriate analytical skills, and as many as 1.5 million people who are able to carry out data analysis.[12]

There is some evidence that the use of this technology can increase margins by as much as 60 percent in corporations. Margin increases of this magnitude are the result of the integration of multiple layers of operations within an organization, including supply-chain management, customer management, after-sales service support, and advertising operations. It is now possible for retailers to gather data in many ways, including through videos of customer shopping patterns, customer reviews of products and services, and direct communication links between retailers and suppliers to monitor inventory levels. It is estimated that there are exabytes of data collected on consumers on a regular basis.[13]

The generational changes that have taken place in this field can be represented by the labels "1.0," "2.0," and "3.0." The beginning of the discipline (1.0) centered on the extraction and storage of data found in relational database management systems, referred to as RDBMS. The use of statistics to analyze data at this level goes back to the 1970s and 1980s. The next stage of development (2.0) centers on the use of analytics that can be found on websites run by eBay and search engines like Google and Yahoo. This level of technological sophistication made it possible for corporations to engage in e-commerce and make a direct connection with their customers. Along with this movement was the ability to analyze qualitative data generated from social media, and to facilitate conversations between organizations and customers via social media. It also enabled organizations to carry out research on the effectiveness of Internet advertising creation and placement. Finally, the emerging future of analytics (3.0) is the application of all of these technological advances to mobile devices, including smartphones and tablets, with the projection that 10 billion mobile devices will be in use by 2020. The beneficiaries of this technology are forecast to be retailers, educators, and manufacturers of gaming devices. This next stage of development focuses on wearable technology, which will create an exponential growth in the amount of data that will be collected.[14]

There are many benefits, opportunities, and risks related to customer data collection and its distribution to third parties. Nowadays, many organizations share their customer data with their business partners. The data have significant value since they may show statistical correlations between purchases of specific products and other customer characteristics that can be used to more precisely target specific messages to a base of customers. In markets across several sectors, companies are using credit histories, sociographic and demographic data, and other types of information to achieve a competitive advantage. Ideally, customer data are collected to improve the customer experience.[15]

A Critical Assessment of the Use of Big Data and Analytics in Politics

These techniques were formally introduced to the political world when Karl Rove, the George W. Bush campaign's chief consultant, determined that the same business tactics used in the commercial world could be applied to politics, ultimately leading Bush to his first victory. That helped the Republican Party to build a database that other candidates were able to use to find likely supporters and avoid wasting time on voters who could not be persuaded.[16]

Throughout both of Obama's victorious presidential campaigns in 2008 and 2012, the use of Big Data was a staple of all decision making. Mark Halperin, a political analyst at *Time* magazine, opined that Obama's 2012 campaign was the most technologically advanced presidential campaign ever run, enabling him to overcome obstacles – such as a weak economy, among other challenges – that might have defeated a less tech-savvy politician. The Obama campaign relied on data mining and social media to communicate with segments of voters who otherwise might have been difficult to contact, especially immigrants. On the other side of the fence, Republicans were never able to achieve a similar level of sophistication in their use of technology.[17]

The Obama team's use of analytics in 2012 resulted in a fivefold increase in staff and resources over 2008.[18] During the 2012 campaign, there was a fair amount of uncertainty among the media with respect to how much influence analytics would actually have on the outcome of the election. In the end however, it turned out that analytics had tremendous predictive capability in forecasting the result. When Obama is compared to the candidates who preceded him in the Democratic Party, it is clear that no other candidate had ever amassed as much sophisticated data on voter attitudes, behavior, demographics, and past voting records as Obama did. Along with this new level of technological sophistication came better targeting of critical segments of voters. The use of this technology by the Obama team gave them the ability to increase registration; make their persuasive techniques more effective with undecided voters; and ultimately achieve a larger voter turnout on election day.[19]

Criticisms of the use of analytics by Obama center on the fact that there is not enough evidence to prove the effectiveness of these efforts. This includes claims by the Obama people that their micro-targeted advertising was more effective than a broad advertising appeal. Furthermore, the point has been made that whereas Obama strategists claimed that they did in fact test as many variables as was humanly possible, many other nontestable variables play a role in the outcome of an election, and with so many nonscientific variables involved, it is hard to isolate the individual effects of each and every variable. The main criticism by those who question the success of the Obama Model is that it is not clear that it can be used as successfully in the future with another presidential candidate. In other words, there are constraints inherent in using these tools that may limit their efficacy.[20]

The Obama Model

In 2008, the Obama team built the largest grassroots organization in the history of American presidential politics. The building process continued over the next several years, making 2008 look almost amateurish by comparison with 2012. Some have argued that Obama did not need the same level of analytic sophistication in 2008 because of the level of excitement in the movement he built, as well as the desire on the part of the American people to move ahead and beyond the Bush years. But in 2012, the polls showed a much closer contest between Obama and Romney than between Obama and McCain in 2008. The Obama team's response was to establish field offices that out-numbered the Romney forces by as many as two to one in critical swing states. Not only were the numbers different, but the actual offices themselves were quite different as well, with Obama's in better neighborhoods, more finished, and simply revealing a polish that the Romney offices lacked.[21]

After Obama's 2008 victory, an organization was created called, "Organizing for America," a group that worked within the Democratic National Committee to continue to use the same marketing tactics to drive the President's agenda. One aspect of its work was the collection of very detailed information about the television viewing habits of key segments of voters. By matching the lists of voters to the names and addresses of cable subscribers, the organizers were able to analyze which channels the voters were using in order to target them with campaign advertisements. By focusing on swing state voters, the campaign came up with a model that assigned a score to voters who were identified as supporters but who needed an additional push to actually come to the polls to vote on election day. This effort, run by Carol Davidsen, was called the "Optimizer" project. As part of this project, the campaign team looked at voters of Latino and African-American descent. They worked with a company called Rentrak, a data firm that tracked the television viewership of these groups of people across more than sixty channels, and they were able to document how their viewing behavior changed every fifteen minutes. In addition, the team could determine the audience size of each group for a specific channel, at a specific time of the day, and then, through a mathematical analysis, target key voters at the lowest possible cost. For example, they were able to identify persuadable voters who lived in households that watch television less than two hours a day. Based on this information, the campaign scheduled ads during the times that these voters were most likely to be watching television. Cost was not an issue for some of these voter segments if they needed them to win a state. They had no choice but to pay the price to get their message across to this key group.[22]

During the course of the 2012 campaign, the Obama team brought together an elite group of data scientists and digital advertising experts who kept secret exactly what they were doing. The chief innovation and integration executive was Michael Slaby, who reiterated that the team was relying less on consumer data and more on voting records that were public documents, as well as responses from workers who were canvassing for the campaign. Furthermore, he said the media were over-emphasizing the team's use of digital tracking records of voters and of cookies to target ads to people who had visited the campaign website, what is referred to as "re-targeting." He revealed also that the web cookies were used to determine if volunteers were in fact reading the online training materials the campaign had prepared. According to Slaby, the campaign's strategic center was a database of registered voters compiled by the Democratic National Committee, which received weekly updates with new public records from election officials in states around the country. In addition to that database, the campaign added its own voter data, something that was kept secret.[23]

The customer database that was amassed in 2012 was the driver of whom to target, whom to telephone, whose door to knock on, which social media channel to use, and the choice of content and message for each. For example, when Sarah Jessica Parker offered her help in the campaign, she was aligned with the people who frequented Reddit. Predictive models were created that allowed political researchers to develop polls with greater accuracy than usual because they knew the predictive accuracy of Obama's polls was rooted in very large states, including key states. Facebook was a very effective tool in the closing days of the campaign, when the Obama team used the website to send e-mails to supporters with names and profile photos of their friends in swing states. Also used were persuasion scores that enabled the campaign to focus its communication efforts and use volunteers manning the telephone banks to contact those voters who were most likely to change their minds. The scores were also used to determine which appeals to put into the ad campaigns. The campaign realized that one telephone call alone might not change a voter's mind, but that several calls might do so. As part of the experimentation that was used to measure the effectiveness of all strategic aspects of the campaign, tests were used to determine how long the persuasion effect lasted after the first phone call; it was about three weeks.[24]

Using Technology to Fine-Tune Product Offerings and Promotional Campaigns

The question now is how this process plays out in other industries, and how the challenges compare to what we witnessed during the two successful campaigns run by Obama. There is no doubt that the right balance must be struck between art and science when using data and technology in developing marketing strategy. According to Barre Hardy, director and research manager of the CMO Agenda initiative at CMG Partners, "One of the biggest surprises to us is how difficult it has been for organizations to find talent who understand both the art and science of marketing and can effectively apply both in their jobs ... Marketers traditionally have been very skilled in the art, and with so much focus on the science of marketing over the last few years, I expected talent to be more available in the market who understand and interpret the science and can apply it to the art of marketing. It seems to be a gap still, although one that is closing."[25]

The MetLife insurance company was working in the dark for some time, not knowing which customers had multiple policies with them, and even lacking the ability to communicate on a regular basis with customers, especially those who were in the middle of a crisis. In 2012, the company implemented a new application called the Wall: Similar to a Facebook application, it provided its sales reps with a profile of customers to use when communicating with them. The new system integrated different databases, bringing up a customer's history with the company. Whereas it had previously taken more than forty clicks on the computer to get access to this kind of information, it now took only one click. Most importantly, as in the Obama campaign, it allowed for real-time decision making, even as customers were navigating the firm's website. MetLife continued with its technology innovation, deciding to put more than $300 million annually into projects that would increase its technological sophistication in an effort to better capture information on its customers. As one MetLife executive put it, "We're a 145-year-old company that's acting like a startup ...

Technology is not just an enabler. It's the fabric of the company – and the future."[26]

Airlines have also begun to invest in technology that allows them to mine the personal data of flyers on their aircraft, enabling them to more accurately target promotions to their customers. It is not surprising to take a seat on an airplane today and find the attendant consulting a tablet computer, looking up data to help respond to flyers' needs – and at the same time continuing to build a customer database. (Again this mirrors how the Obama team were able to accurately direct the plethora of e-mail, text, and other Internet messages to the appropriate supporters.) In fact, online browsing histories of flyers give the airlines an insight into other likes and dislikes of their flyers, often without the flyer knowing the information is being collected. According to Maya Leibman, chief technology and information officer for American Airlines, "data is key to almost everything we're doing." Although this technology is not new to many for-profit industries, what is unique about the airline industry is the amount of information that can be obtained – about food preferences, for example, among many other things.[27]

Up until recently, airlines relied on older technology, where various databases were held in separate areas, such as loyalty programs, bookings, and so on. This was before the era of Big Data, where the capabilities to bring diverse data sets together now exist. This now makes it possible for airlines to amalgamate data sets using different types of passenger identification, such as e-mail addresses, frequent flier numbers, and so on. So the possibility now exists for an attendant on the airline to have access instantaneously to all of this information on a tablet, or even a smartphone. For the airlines, the real bottom line is that they can now identify who their "top" customers are based on the historical data they have. This could result not only in better service and treatment for those customers but also in a "touch-point" that can be leveraged to offer promotions to keep customers loyal. In addition, the airlines are able to determine how their revenue streams are divided up among alternative offerings. Some people have questioned the usefulness of this information, given that many passengers are simply interested in getting the best seat possible, and do not care whether the attendant knows that they drink a particular cocktail during flight, or have specific food preferences. United Airlines uses the information to target fliers who would likely be willing to pay for an upgrade to economy-plus from economy seating. In one application that turned out to be a negative for British Airlines (which has one of the more sophisticated databases), frequent fliers were being identified and greeted by name at the gate based on images culled from the airline's website. This turned out to be a bit too personal for some of these passengers, and the practice was stopped. The point is that each organization has unique and different ways of using technology, depending on the nature of what is being sold, how often the organization comes into contact with its customers, and the requirements and constraints imposed by privacy issues.[28]

JetBlue Airways Corporation is also very involved in the digital movement, mainly focused on their advertising. Working with several different technology consulting firms, it has put out a full court press to get its message out to customers and potential customers via their computers and on their mobile devices. The firms that the company is working with operate in different areas of the digital advertising world, including firms that are focused on geo-targeting, companies that track and interpret what people are saying about companies on social networks, consulting firms that enable a firm to customize ad content on the basis of how customers are browsing on websites, and companies that specialize in enabling communication via mobile telephones. The degree of specialization in this hi-tech area can center on working with firms to aggregate space across a series of sites and resell it to companies like JetBlue, and also to track where ads have run to verify the advertising purchases that companies make. One particular ad buy made by JetBlue included television ads, social-media promotions on Twitter, as well as mobile spots. American Airlines has worked with clickstream technology, an advanced system that allows a company to record everything a user does while navigating on a company's website. This has helped the airline to determine what may drive customers either to purchase a ticket on American or to take their business elsewhere. Hadoop, the specific data technology being used by American, records all information for a limited number of users on their website, including the amount of time a user's cursor sits on particular part of the computer screen. If a person then leaves the site without making a purchase, Hadoop can track where that same customer went to next on the web. As with the system employed by Facebook, Hadoop relies on software that runs on clusters of low-cost servers, allowing it to manage large amounts of information.[29]

Text Analytics is a company that uses digital branding. For many companies, it is a challenge to process data, and they need people who understand the language of technology. Text Analytics relies on the use of patterns and trends to form conclusions about information that is generated by texts. One example of this is "sentiment analysis," a system that allows a company to predict trends based on the attitudes of users communicated on social media. Unfortunately, this process is not completely accurate because it doesn't take into account the role of words that reflect sarcasm or even nonverbal messages. In the same way that predictive models rely on a customer's past behavior to forecast future behavior, text analytics can help companies infer similar insights by analyzing more subtle text patterns to respond to customer questions. This technology allows a company to get a better understanding of the online behavior of customers. For example, as more and more people interact online, their interaction evolves in different ways. Companies consequently need to use more sophisticated tools to understand the patterns in this interaction – in effect, to "read between the lines" of what customers are saying – as the conversations that take place strongly influence how a company uses the information gathered to empower the customer.[30]

Government and Nonprofit Use of Technology

One of the most important players to use technology is the government! As different types of social media become more and more important and are used by more people, leaders in government realize they are an avenue through which to keep a strong link to and communication channel with constituents. In an effort to educate governments on this issue, GovDelivery and EfficientGov hosted a webinar to outline the best practices for digital communication, identified by these companies as a result of working with hundreds of public sector organizations around the world. The argument put forward by the companies was tied into the fact that governments continue to face the need for budget cuts, making it more difficult for them to take on any projects that cannot guarantee a positive return on the investment. Some of the conclusions from the webinar, and those which have application to the marketing of any technological advance in any industry, included the following: Make it easy to sign up; keep on promoting it; keep on assessing it; automate as much as you can; harness the data by using and integrating both quantitative and qualitative sources of information; and find ways to get people to pay attention to it.[31]

As one compares the use of technology by the Obama team as a campaign tool with its use as governing tool – for example, in implementing

Obama's healthcare plan – there are some stark differences. For one, there was the difference in magnitude of the players involved. The Obama team during each of the two campaigns was run by a few key players, whereas the rollout of healthcare.gov included more than fifty different contractors. Second, the rollout process was full of red tape and bureaucracy and the subject of intense political pressure from parties both inside and outside government who opposed the plan. The Obama team as a campaign juggernaut did not face that kind of opposition. Third, the rollout committed the ultimate crime in the world of software development in the business world – a lack of transparency – as the code was kept secret, not allowing other experts to point out flaws in the program. In fact, the Obama executives in charge of this rollout were accused of a lack of responsibility for not inviting Silicon Valley experts to work with them.[32]

Super PACs (mega-political action committees), nonprofit organizations that support different political candidates during the course of a campaign, are primarily funded by large contributions from a small number of donors. In the 2010 case of *Citizens United v. Federal Election Commission*, the Supreme Court ruled that the federal government could not limit the donations made to political action committees, resulting in a sharp increase in the domination of the contributions by a few very wealthy donors. One of the more well-known examples was the $10 million contribution by casino magnate Sheldon Adelson to Newt Gingrich's cash-strapped operation at one point during the Republican primaries. These organizations are relying on the same advanced technological methods as for-profit organizations.[33]

There are more than 1 million nonprofit organizations in the United States, and to succeed, each of them is forced to rely on the same tactics used by corporations in the for-profit sector, including use of many of the marketing technology tools that have been re-invented by the Obama campaign. Nonprofit organizations must rely on the use of technology to recruit and maintain support by volunteers and donors. All of this is carried out in an effort to create and build the kind of long-term relationships that have become the mainstay of the for-profit sector, and, as described earlier in this chapter, that were implemented successfully by the Obama team in 2008 and 2012. Ultimately, all good marketing campaigns must be long on good ideas and effective implementation and short on errors, especially when the campaign is driven online. The Obama campaign team was careful to plot its moves one step at a time, and always worked to capitalize on what the competition was doing. The ability to conduct a campaign that ran as efficiently as both of Obama's hinged on their creative use of technology.

During the 2008 campaign, the Obama team predicted that the American people would come to see his administration as "the iPod government." Some have argued that Obama was comfortable with technology in a way that no president before him had been. It was part of his goal to pull the federal government into the digital age. Obama followed through with this initiative by creating the positions of chief information officer and chief technology officer in the White House. He also created an online dashboard to allow anyone interested to observe how the government was using these technologies. Unfortunately for the Obama team in 2013, the failure of the launch of the online portal to deliver on the Affordable Care Act – which was supposed to be a model for the delivery of social programs in the twenty-first century – represented something of a "black eye" for the use of technology in government.[34]

Chapter Four

Lesson 3: Integrate Research Methods

One of the most important areas of inquiry in any marketing campaign centers on the choice of research methods. In marketing any product or service, all strategy must ultimately depend on the use of research to carry out and implement the chosen course of action. The argument of this book is that the marketing concept is a driving force in all organizations, establishing the need to carry out research to understand the needs and wants of a targeted group of people, be they citizens or voters or consumers. Further questions concern which groups of people should be investigated and which are the best research methods to use in carrying out that investigation.

It is essential for an organization to understand the importance of using the correct methods to gather information, especially in relation to selected segments of the population. Given that a presidential campaign will be won or lost through the decisions of people young and old, we cannot minimize the significance of the difference between a young college student versus a seventy-year-old when it comes to voting. The older voter is probably getting political information from the evening news on network television stations, while the college student is probably getting political news from websites downloaded through apps on a mobile phone or laptop.

Qualitative versus Quantitative Research Methods

In both 2008 and 2012, the Obama campaigns relied heavily on several different types of research methods, all of which were coordinated in an integrative manner to ensure maximum synergy among the different types of procedures. Broadly speaking, research methods fall into two categories – "qualitative" and "quantitative." A wide variety of methods exist to collect and analyze data in both categories. The use of both qualitative and quantitative research tools generates descriptive and behavioral sources of information, allowing an organization to profile important segments of customers (or voters) as well as to target them with appropriate appeals that will result in behavior beneficial to the organization. It should be noted that while quantitative analysis involves the use of numbers, it also relies on the use of words (a qualitative orientation) to make the correct interpretation of the results. Similarly, qualitative methods often rely on quantitative information to make a correct interpretation. In short, rather than being independent approaches to the use of technology, the two are complementary methodologies that support and enhance one another.[1]

A Brief History of Political Research Methods

Most of the research on the voting behavior of citizens has focused on investigative studies carried out in various social science fields.[2] The oldest studies on voting behavior, using what is referred to as the socio-structural method, date back to the early 1940s, when the thinking was that the most important motivation for voters was their sense of belonging to a community – professional, religious, or of some other type.[3] Much of the research during that period centered on collecting data on various socio-economic variables that described citizens, and then looking aggregately at a particular group's voting patterns. These pioneering studies began with the presidential elections in 1940 when Franklin D. Roosevelt ran against Wendell Willkie. A follow-up set of studies was carried out during the 1948 presidential election, when Harry Truman ran against Thomas Dewey. Voting behavior researchers at this time determined that choosing a presidential candidate was the result of a group process, usually following the influence of families (which were considered to be most influential), neighbors, and other people known as opinion leaders whom citizens looked up to for direction. At this time, the media were not thought to play a significant role in voters' decisions. Certainly, that would change over the course of many presidential elections in the United States.

Research carried out some decades after the work of these pioneering studies looked at another very important predictor of voting, which is party identification.[4] The results of these studies concluded that during the course of a campaign, voters knew who they were going to cast a ballot for and could not be influenced by the efforts of competing candidates. Data collected during this period also began to focus on the importance of understanding whether voters had made up their minds and on how to translate this information into strategies directed at two key segments of voters – decided and undecided.[5] The thinking was that voters who had made up their minds long before the campaign had a sense of belonging to a particular group and would be resistant to the efforts of a competing candidate to change their minds. Last-minute deciders, however, were thought not to have a similar sense of belonging; moreover, while in theory they should be more open to the influence of the media, they might not be, simply because of low interest. Furthermore, while party identification still matters in politics, the two Obama campaigns suggest that research should be focused on issues as well as party identification, since the latter has been documented as of declining importance as a predictor of voter behavior, with the designation "independent" becoming more meaningful for many citizens who are asked to classify themselves.[6]

The Use of Focus Groups by Political Organizations

One of the most commonly used qualitative research methods is known as a focus group, where between ten and fifteen individuals are invited to respond to questions about new product ideas and various other strategic issues of concern to executives. During his two presidential campaigns, Obama tweaked this process and eliminated the need to pay as much for these services by relying on more informal gatherings of citizens. In the process of building these relationships, he was able to engage in his "listening" campaign to find out what was on the minds of individual supporters. This was of course critically important to the Obama team in its effort to bring to the polls the voters who supported him. One of Obama's campaign operatives talked about the importance of finding out what people care about so that, when Obama spoke to them, he was able to keep their attention. This is something that corporations have also been engaged in for many years now, though not in such a cost-effective way. Initially, Obama needed to identify the issues of concern to his supporters to be able to use quantitative analysis – the other important research tool – to test and determine the significance of all issues.[7]

The use of focus groups by politicians is a fixture in both the political and business worlds. The real benefit of focus groups, according to some research companies, is their ability to bring out the "emotion" behind statements made by people, whether they are consumers or voters. A poll, on the other hand, can be tested for validity and reliability (two important tests used by researchers to see if in fact what is being asked in the poll is in fact being measured, and how consistent the results are across different questions), which will measure how accurate the poll was. Hence, the use of qualitative research, such as a focus group, is more of an "art," whereas the use of quantitative research falls under the heading of a "science."[8]

Qualitative research is used to try to identify those hot-button issues that may come out of a focus group and lead to a multimillion-dollar advertising campaign that wins the election for a candidate. A case in point was the 1988 contest between George H.W. Bush and Michael Dukakis. During that campaign, Bush operatives ran focus groups to help isolate exactly what it would take to switch Dukakis supporters over to Bush. What came out of the focus groups was the importance of being tough on crime-related issues. It became clear to the Bush strategists on the basis of this qualitative data that Dukakis voters would switch their allegiance from Dukakis to Bush if they determined that Dukakis was soft on crime.

Further investigation led to the story of one inmate in prison in Massachusetts, William "Willie" Horton, a convicted felon who, while serving a life sentence for murder (without any possibility of parole), was furloughed for a weekend through a program available to some of the most hardened criminals. As it turned out, Mr. Horton did not return to prison on time, and while he was out, he committed an armed robbery and raped a woman. At the time, Bush's campaign manager, Lee Atwater, said, "By the time we're finished, they're going to wonder whether Willie Horton is Dukakis's running mate."[9] The resulting commercial showed a felon walking through a revolving door, going into prison and then getting let out, implying that the governor of the state, Michael Dukakis, was soft on crime. The ad had a great impact and eventually killed his chances to win.

Another interesting and well-known case of a focus group that led to a winning advertising strategy took place during the 1984 Democratic primaries when pollster Peter Hart was working for Walter Mondale. After Senator Gary Hart handily beat Vice-president Walter Mondale in the New Hampshire primary, Peter Hart was given the task of finding out why Hart had beaten Mondale so decisively, in order to develop a strategy for the next primary state, Georgia. In several focus groups,

Peter Hart asked the focus group attendees to imagine that the country was in a terrible recession, with unemployment running very high, and then to decide whom they would like to see as president. Overwhelmingly, they all said Gary Hart, because he was perceived to be young and vibrant and capable of leading the country in tough times, whereas Walter Mondale was perceived to be old and tired. So Peter then presented another hypothetical scenario, where the country was in the midst of an international crisis, and the "red phone" (which is only used in international crises) started to ring. He asked who they would like to see answer that phone, Gary Hart or Walter Mondale. The answer was overwhelmingly Mondale. When pushed to explain, they all said that Hart was untested and too young. Not long after that, a commercial was put into place in Georgia with the red phone playing a prominent role, and it led to a Mondale victory there. The same red phone commercial was used in states around the country as the primary season progressed, and Gary Hart never was able to respond to the commercial with one of his own, eventually losing the nomination to Mondale.[10]

The Use of Polling in Politics

Quantitative analysis offers insights about voters to candidates in the same way it has for many years helped corporations to understand what influences the actions of thousands of consumers, examining responses to survey questions using multivariate statistical analysis to find trends and issues that unite seemingly disparate groups around a particular issue. In contrast to qualitative research, statistical analysis seeks to model some aspect of reality, like an election that will take place at some point in the future, and forecast the result of that election based on data collected from thousands of voters. Most people understand that this is carried out in politics through polling, which if done correctly, enables the researcher to forecast the behavior of hundreds of thousands of voters based on responses from as few as a thousand people. This is possible through the use of sampling procedures and advanced statistical analysis. In effect, the researcher is forecasting on the basis of observation and data collection and analysis, identifying indicators of individual preferences and testing them on many people – be it consumers who are loyal to a particular brand in the marketplace or a segment of voters who are loyal to a candidate – to determine if they are widespread.

The purpose behind political polling is to accurately forecast the results of a future election. Traditional polls, like the Harris or Gallup polls, which have been used for decades, are getting competition from new polls that aggregate their predictions across many different individual polls. When this new type of poll was used by Nate Silver during the 2012 presidential campaign, he accurately predicted the winner in every state. This has been referred to as the new "state of the art" poll that takes into the account the unique features of individual polls and accounts for them statistically in the model that is built.[11] This of course raises a very important point that centers on the timing of the poll, with polls conducted too far in advance of an election being less accurate than those that are conducted very close to the election.[12]

Another model developed for forecasting election results has been put forward by two researchers, one from Google (Patrick Hummel), and the other from Microsoft Research (David Rothschild), both of whom were formerly at Yahoo! Research. Their model used data from previous elections (hundreds of them), combining that with other historical data such as economic indicators, presidential approval ratings, characteristics of the candidates running in a campaign, and the length of time a party had been in power, each of which was broken down into variables that were used in a simple linear regression statistical model comprising approximately 100,000 pieces of data. In February 2012, they accurately predicted the number of electoral votes Obama and Romney would get in all states except for Florida. They make a distinction between what they did and the use of Big Data, which can incorporate as many as tens of billions of pieces of data in any single analysis. The 2012 campaign was the first election for which economists were able to make these predictions, in part because of the development of computers that could handle the analysis, in part because of algorithms developed around the time of the campaign.[13]

The Obama Model

The use of both quantitative and qualitative research in political campaigns offers an approach to the study of decision making, in this case by voters, that demonstrates some creative uses of research not seen before the Obama teams used them in 2008 and 2012. The two Obama campaigns made innovative use of both the qualitative and quantitative approaches – as will be described in detail here. Some have argued that differences in the use of the two analytical approaches on the commercial side ties into the culture of a company. Some have argued further that not only do the approaches represent different cultures, but that groups favoring one approach may be very suspicious of the value of the other approach. This is one area where the Obama team excelled, incorporating an integrative approach that benefited from both "cultures."[14] Both qualitative and quantitative methods were used extensively in both of the Obama victories, including polling, consumer research, marketing research, database development, focus groups, benchmark and follow-up polls, tracking polls, and other innovative research tools – all used to collect information on voters.

What the Obama team was most sophisticated at doing was integrating the function of each of the different methods in a complementary fashion. Research methods used during both campaigns showed a high level of skill in integrating different types of research from many different sources gathered over a long period. For example, real-time decisions on messages that popped up on the campaign website were based on new technologies that allowed the campaign to choose the most effective way to connect with and respond to interested parties. Messages sent out in different vehicles, whether by e-mail, text, or on television, were arrived at through an experimentation process that helped to shape not only the message used but the frequency with which it was delivered. (One thing that surprised the Obama team in charge of sending out e-mail messages was the lack of negative reaction to repeated messages, sometimes sent more than once a day, such as requests for money and volunteer help at critical junctures in the campaign. These rarely led to a request for any previous donor to be taken off of the list of recipients.) Research was carried out extensively throughout both campaigns (but especially in 2012) to monitor the effectiveness of the different appeals used.

During Obama's 2008 campaign, Peter Hart carried out several focus groups to get a better understanding of the electorate. With twelve people attending one of the sessions, all of whom were paid $100, they were selected very carefully, with six Democrats, two independents who leaned Democratic, two Republicans, and two totally independent voters. All of the attendees indicated that they did not support either Obama or McCain before an upcoming primary, but seven had voted for Hillary Clinton in a previous primary campaign, and Peter Hart's interest was to see how the Clinton supporters felt about Obama. The conclusion of this focus group was that the campaign was pretty wide open at the time of the Pennsylvania primary. While McCain did not come out looking very strong, it was clear that the race between Obama and Clinton could go either way.[15]

The more advanced technologies in the political sphere have moved the field beyond what was the best route to getting feedback from voters via opinion polls and marketing research surveys to more hi-tech routes that rely on social networks. These networks facilitate the interaction between citizens and political organizations, increasing the amount of communication between both groups. During the 2008 election, Obama built what would become the largest single database of citizens who were willing to support their favorite Democratic candidate with both money and volunteer time. When the 2012 campaign started, Obama had five times as many Twitter followers and eight times as many Facebook followers as all of the Republican candidates put together.

The use of qualitative and quantitative data by political organizations has established a trend that will likely be followed by organizations in many different industries for decades to come. The recent Obama campaigns have ushered in a new world for Super PACs, which are now able to target key voters in swing states with the use of advanced technological tools tested in 2008 and perfected in 2012. Right-wing Super PACs worked directly with teams of workers from Facebook, Twitter, and Google to try and turn Obama out of office. Internet-based advertising is being employed through the use of these tools to get out their message. In fact Google had three separate teams of campaigners working on the 2012 election: One worked with the Democratic campaigns; one with the Republicans; and a third one with what were described as the independent groups, mainly Super PACs.[16]

Collecting Data through Social Media

From the point of view of the retailer, collecting the appropriate information must center on the movement of people from the social media site to the website and eventually to the retail location. Building traffic on social media sites can be used to similarly build traffic on a company's website and retail location. It should be made clear that the same methods are not necessarily used for all social media sites. For example, the strategy used for Facebook is very different from the one used for Twitter, and is different again for Google+, Pinterest, Instagram, and other sites. Depending on the type of business a company is engaged in, some social media platforms will work better than others. This is where the merging of the worlds of qualitative and quantitative research comes into play. Analytics must be matched with the social media site to determine which posts get the most engagement from visitors, something that can only be determined from a qualitative analysis. For example, it may be better to post over a weekend when there is not as much competition for the attention of your visitors. The time of day a posting is made also makes a difference. All of this information must be analyzed quantitatively, then subjected to content analyses to arrive at the appropriate strategic conclusions. The Obama team in 2012 used an extensive "trial-and-error" methodology to determine which e-mail messages resonated better with receivers, and the same strategy should be employed when using social media in the commercial marketplace.[17]

The use of quantitative methods allows for the use of trial-and-error procedures to arrive at the best strategy. Using responses from more than 23,000 online consumers, the J.D. Power and Associates 2013 Social Media Benchmark Study sought to measure the overall consumer experience in using a social media outlet in their purchase and service behavior. The study looked at over 100 U.S. brands in six different sectors, including the automobile, credit card, telecom, utilities, airline, and banking industries. The study offered insights into how best to use social media and the research results from the study. By focusing on the use of servicing versus marketing activities on social media, the researchers arrived at two key conclusions. First, they found different levels of engagement with social marketing interaction depending on the age of the individual, with younger people (18–29) interacting more than older individuals (over 50). Second, they concluded that there is an overall satisfaction correlation between a company's social marketing activities and consumers' perception of the company.

Some Findings about the Use of Social Media as a Source of Data

One company that is documenting the growth of this kind of data is the Nielsen Company, which released a report in 2012 on the growth of this evolving technology, especially in the nonprofit area. The key findings were that social media are here to stay. Facebook is clearly ahead of the rest of the group of companies in this industry. It is now slightly over a decade since this new movement started, and it is clear that there is a consistent growth trend in this area, with new and innovative entrants coming onto the scene on a regular basis, including more recent offerings like Pinterest and Snapchat. In 2012, while LinkedIn showed very little growth, Pinterest showed the most significant movement, with a 1,047 percent year-over-year change. Even though Facebook is not growing at a similar pace, it continues to maintain its sizable lead in market share over other social networks.[18]

The growth in mobile technology, which seriously began to take hold in 2012, will enhance the effectiveness of this new technology from a database perspective, something that will become a key factor in political campaigns beginning with the 2016 U.S. presidential election. As compared to growth in the use of mobile devices, PC use is still growing but at a much slower rate. However, computers are still the most popular device for using social media, with Nielsen reporting that 61 percent of total social media time spent online takes place in front of a computer. So how do these statistics play into the hand of organizations that want to collect data from their current and potential customers, as well as from other organizations that they may see as competitive threats? And why is it important to measure and document this movement? Because, according to the Nielsen report, 70 percent of social media users indicate that they are hearing about other people's experiences with a specific brand or an organization at least once a month. This kind of information needs to be measured on both a quantitative and a qualitative level. In addition, according to results from the same report, 53 percent of social media users had something positive to say about brands they use, while 50 percent said they shared a complaint. This means that without a database that documents both the degree and type of comments, companies will not be in a competitive position to harness such information as they develop strategies. Finally, the Nielsen report also discussed the rise in "social care," or the degree to which customer service is accessed online as opposed to over the telephone. They report that 33 percent of social media users prefer to receive help online as opposed to over the telephone.[19]

Social Media Data Collection by Nonprofit Organizations

Nonprofit companies are relying on social media in a way that is unprecedented. In a recent survey of small organizations, it turns out that they use social media in similar ways as for-profit companies do, but with a few twists. First of all, there are more nonprofits than small businesses on Facebook (96 percent versus 90 percent). Second, nonprofits are more active on Facebook than small businesses (76 percent post multiple times per week versus 66 percent of small businesses). Finally, whereas both nonprofits and small businesses report that posting content is a very time-consuming activity, nonprofits indicate that responding to questions on social media is also very time-consuming.[20]

One of the biggest organizations in the world, the Vatican, is also relying on the use of both qualitative and quantitative technological tools. When Pope Benedict XVI stepped down as pontiff, he had already put digital programs into place at the Vatican, among them a Twitter account that allows more than 2 million people to follow the Pope's activities. This is just the most visible of his technological initiatives. One important lesson from the Vatican's decision to use technology as a bridge to connect with followers concerned the possible negative effects of such a move. According to Monsignor Paul Tighe, a Vatican insider who worked to integrate social media with other media at the Vatican, a strong reaction was anticipated, on both the positive and the negative side. As it turns out, all tweets sent out by the @Pontifex account had to be approved by the Pope himself, which inevitably led to time lags in delivering responses. In the words of one advisor, "I think that's part of our challenge … Institutions, be they governmental or church, are often risk averse. We don't like making mistakes in public. And yet, if you are to speak the language, you are not going to learn it until you try speaking it. One of the things important for us is trying different things, working with different things and, through receptivity and feedback, learning to make it better." [21]

Labor Unions also Rely on Both Qualitative and Quantitative Data

The Democratic Party over the years has learned a lot from the labor movement's use of innovations in organizing supporters to get out the vote and donate money and time. However, one difference between the use of research by the labor unions versus the Obama team was the fact that the labor movement has relationships with a network of people who already share an ideology, as opposed to people who only potentially do so.[22]

For many years now, unions have been collecting information on their own members, integrating the most updated databases with the large volume of data on many different industries in an effort to organize their members to carry out strategic campaigns on issues as they arise in different states around the country. For example, workplace grievances were used as an effective way to mobilize members. These databases include both quantitative and qualitative information that has helped unions to choose particular leaders with specific talents who had been successful in past movements. This kind of integration served as a model for the Democratic Party as it sought to build on the technical expertise developed by the labor movement for use in electoral campaigns. The one dimension of this kind of data collection by unions that has not been measured is its contribution to effective organizing on the part of unions. The only measure of success has been the voting behavior of union members. Statistical models like those used during the Obama presidential campaigns have not been put in place. One could argue that a statistical model is not a substitute for the use of talented, dedicated organizers; however, it is clear that the unions' database-building process is incomplete.[23]

Important Issues to Consider When Integrating Research Methods

One of the key research methods used to collect data during a presidential campaign is the focus group. In fact, as described earlier in this chapter, it is used as a methodology by all kinds of organizations to gain insights into the thinking and behavior of voters and consumers. However, there are some specific guidelines that should be followed if an organization is going to take advantage of the lessons revealed through the Obama campaigns. Careful attention needs to be given to how these groups are selected, formed, and conducted depending on the industry that is using them. When considering using focus groups for marketing research, a marketer should be mindful of several issues. The feedback from a focus group is easily influenced by the makeup of the group, the size of the group, and the questions asked. The focus group represents a good example of how bias can interfere with the pursuit of better information about your customer, whether it is a voter or a consumer.

One of the most valuable aspects of focus group research is that participants often provide insights, reactions, and opinions that were completely unexpected by the researcher. Even if a focus group is conducted and assembled properly to remove all potential biases, the insights provided should not necessarily be used to justify action. While focus groups are valuable in that they provide qualitative data that would be difficult to gather otherwise, these data may need further analysis. If a focus group provides an insight into a pain point of interacting with a product, rather than using this insight as a mandate for R & D to alter the design, the researcher should instead attempt to quantify the data in a further study with a more statistically relevant sample. Whether information is obtained through data mining or through survey research, many times there seem to be overwhelming trends within a data set. Focus groups are an ideal way to dive into quantitative data.

In quantitative research, having a representative sample is the most important factor in ensuring the validity of data. However, in a focus group environment one has to consider the group dynamic and the effects it has on the data that are emerging. In focus groups, homogeneity is a desired characteristic, so that group members can leverage their shared experiences in a way that is productive and cumulative. Obvious disparities in status could greatly influence the group's dynamic and could create exaggerated answers or discourage participation. When using a focus group as the main outlet to collect qualitative data, therefore, it is not critical that the groups be a representative sample, whereas in quantitative data collection representativeness is essential if one is going to draw conclusions about a particular population. The size of the focus group is also important. Research indicates that the larger the group the less personal pressure the participants feel to contribute. This can create a bias in the data based on contributions from a few members who dominate or guide the data. If a researcher values the insights of each member of the focus group, the researcher should strive to create groups of a size where each member feels valued and thus compelled to participate.[24]

Technology Drives Research

The use of both qualitative and quantitative data in all marketing campaigns will certainly continue to be an integral part of strategy development in all industries in the future. As mentioned earlier in the chapter, the purposes for the use of different research methods are sector-specific, but there is no doubt that technology will play a key role in how they are integrated. The PC is still the hub of the communication network for most people, but with more and more people using smart phones and tablets on a regular basis, there is a movement toward mobile usage, making the integration with social media websites more accessible in new ways that will challenge the ability of companies to integrate databases. Time spent on mobile apps accounts for close to two-thirds of the growth in overall time spent using social media. Forty-five percent of social media users indicate that they use their smart phone to access social media.[25]

New social media sites continue to grow and get the funding of venture capitalists, as demonstrated by the number of new IPOs in this industry. Social media are now being used by more and more people to witness and experience events around the world – from debates in U.S. presidential elections to the summer Olympics to emerging global crises – and to share their reactions with friends and family. The potential for data collection as a result of this movement is huge, a virtual gold mine of information available to political campaigns, for-profit companies, and nonprofit organizations alike, its value dependent only on their ability to harness that information and package it in appropriate formats.[26]

According to Nielsen and NM Incite's 2012 Social Media Report, there will be a continued drive for all organizations to understand the obsession with the social media, especially in light of the following statistics: one-third of social media users find ads on social networking sites to be harder to ignore than other types of Internet advertisements. More than 25 percent of social media users also indicate that they are more likely to pay attention to an ad shared by one of their social friends. Finally, over 25 percent of consumers actually like the idea of seeing ads that are tailored to their profile on social networks.[27]

Marketers have known for many years that word-of-mouth communication is the most effective means of influencing other people's opinions, simply because one assumes that, unlike a commercial enterprise, an individual does not have an ax to grind. Hence, as global-word-of-mouth increasingly becomes more prevalent, the ability to manage that phenomenon becomes more important. Citizens and consumers possess more power as a result of these new technologies. Whereas most people in the past were limited to influencing people they knew personally, now it is possible to influence hundreds, maybe thousands, maybe even millions of people who follow one person's thinking. How can that flow of information be tracked and accumulated into databases? Political organizations have figured this out, and it is something that both nonprofit and for-profit companies will need to better understand in the future.

Chapter Five

Lesson 4: Develop a Unique Brand Identity

All corporations understand the need to develop a unique identity but may not know how to present all of their products and services as a single, unified brand. Obama figured this out and used it to communicate a clear message to voters during both of his campaigns, sometimes using fear appeals in a competitive manner, and at other times relying on psychological mechanisms that influenced voters in a desired direction. This also called for the careful development of campaign slogans, logos, and colors that were coordinated strategically.

According to many marketers of commercial products, brand plays an important – even critical – role in the decision-making process of a consumer. However, marketers are beginning to observe noticeable differences in consumer behavior with regard to brand loyalty and positioning. "In the past, consumers had no way of accurately assessing the real quality of things directly, so they usually evaluated quality based on generic, top-of-mind reference points and quality proxies. One such proxy was the brand name. But brands are less needed when consumers can assess product quality using better sources of information such as reviews from other users, expert opinion, or information from people they know on social media. Reassured by the opinions of others, consumers are less hesitant to try a lesser known brand."[1]

Brands serve a very fundamental role for customers, which is to simplify their choices in the marketplace on a daily basis. The role of the brand manager includes many functions, including the following: positioning the brand; integrating the marketing carried out for the brand; assessing the performance of the brand; and growing and managing the brand. The positioning of a brand centers on creating a linkage in the mind of the customer that gives a company a competitive edge.[2]

A very major role of branding is to create emotional connections with the customer – often through a narrative that connects the customer with the brand in question. This calls for the use of tactics that are based on a deep understanding of the users of a brand. The emergence of emotional branding occurred in the late 1990s, superseding an earlier focus on benefits. With the increasingly important role of social media in all branding campaigns, this approach has become even more popular as customers rely on their social networks to express their feelings about companies and their products and services.[3]

In the political marketplace, a candidate's success depends on the candidate's ability to create a brand that is received and understood by the public across all groups, regardless of demography or socio-economic status. At the very least, the brand needs to be perceived as consistent in its motives, messaging, and responses to circumstances as they unfold. A brand that is consistent and whose messages are received in the way they are intended is a brand that can be trusted. This trust translates most importantly into predictability. The dreaded "flip-flopping" politician is perceived as untrustworthy. Thus, the public will feel as though they are unable to predict how a candidate will react to crises they will inevitably face while in office. Through effective branding, a candidate can assuage the uncertainty of the public and through consistent messaging earn a reputation as predictable and trustworthy. This chapter examines the 2008 and 2012 presidential elections to determine what role in shaping the candidate's successes and failures branding, loyalty, and positioning played, while also considering how the adoption and use of emerging social media platforms reinforced a brand.

Defining Your Brand

The literature on branding includes many different definitions of "brand," but most revolve around the notion that a brand can have both a symbolic (or emotional) and an economic connection with the customer.[4] These same attributes of a brand can be extended to political candidates, who may connect with voters via the policies and issues they represent as well as through the personality traits they possess. At the same time, other celebrities in society also represent brands that are attractive to people. For example, Lebron James, who has emerged as one of the leading NBA stars and who decided to move from the Miami Heat back to Cleveland with the hopes of bringing a championship to his hometown Cleveland Cavaliers, is a brand. So is Barack Obama, and so is the iPhone, and so is any recognizable company that has established a unique identity in the public's mind – such as McDonald's or Sony, for example. What is the role of a brand? "Creating a compelling brand message, of course, is no easy task. But failing to create your own narrative allows opponents to create it for you. A unified campaign story is essential to unify voters around a single moment in history."[5] If a brand is a promise, then creating a brand is equivalent to earning the trust of the public. Without the trust of the public, a promise is empty words. A promise merely communicates, at best, good intentions, and at worst, when not delivered upon, a perception of an attempt to manipulate. Building a brand that can be trusted is key, but the crafting and management of the message a brand conveys are even more important. In 2008, the Obama slogan "Change We Can Believe In" seemed to communicate a message of opposition to politics as we have come to know it. It acknowledged the idea that promises are often made to the American people but rarely delivered on, and Obama's campaign sought to set him apart both from the incumbent, President George W. Bush, and the other contender, John McCain, by implying they were not to be believed. By having an established brand image, a company or politician can create a type of loyalty that will allow a customer or voter to consciously dismiss competitors' attempts to redefine the brand. This raises the critical question of the tactics used to communicate a brand in the marketplace.

Branding and Communication

As with other strategic marketing tools, the role of branding is changing as a result of the technological advances that have taken place over the past several years. This is also the result of consumers who demand and expect companies to communicate with them in a style and manner they are comfortable with. This transformation, described by some as a change from modernism to postmodernism, reflects a shift in society, resulting in a movement from objective, universal laws to more subjective interpretations and lack of universal orientations. Specifically, this is the result of the role of digital media that some argue have transformed the way people communicate. The question is, what is the challenge to organizations? The answer is a highly interactive situation that brings together one consumer with another, as well as connecting the consumer with a company through multiple media outlets. This fluidity makes it more important than ever before to have a well-defined brand identity that can be clearly communicated. With the consumer playing a more active role in shaping what information is received about a brand, the result is what some have referred to as a postmodern orientation that is having a big influence on organizations of all types.[6]

Brands need to be communicated to consumers on multiple levels, one of which is the value a brand acquires as a function of who is currently using it, which is referred to as "network effects." However, for some companies, network effects create barriers to entry for companies with new brands.[7] What continues to play a key role in the branding of a product is the way in which consumers perceive the organization that sells it. This is especially important for nonprofit organizations that sometimes have to deal with the issue of a negative impact on a brand when management is accused of mishandling a situation – for example, when an employee of a charitable organization misappropriates funds targeted to a particular group. What is imperative is to understand the stakeholders who hold perceptions of an organization's brands, and to reflect those perceptions as opposed to those of third parties.[8]

The reality is that many companies do not have a clear marketing strategy, making it difficult to accurately communicate the essence of a brand to customers. All brand communications must be based on a marketing strategy in order to develop the correct value propositions, and this must then be followed up with tactics to properly communicate the value proposition to the customer. This is where the distinction between strategy and tactics exists, with strategy determining the value proposition and tactics focusing on a specific set of benefits or attributes that the customer uses to make a choice in the marketplace. To be successful with the communication of a brand, a company must always begin with a definition of the needs of their customers, followed by a definition of the goals of the company, followed by the development of tactics that can be translated into a set of best practices to follow. In addition, without a careful timeline for carrying out the identified tactics, it becomes difficult to measure the success of the brand.[9]

An organization needs to understand the difference between strategy and tactics when it comes to successfully communicating the value of a brand to customers. Although it is important to first develop a strategy before tactics can be implemented, it is equally important to have a good grasp of your competition and the positioning of their brands in the marketplace. It is not enough to run a social media campaign along with other promotional campaigns in more traditional outlets without having a clear idea of how they should work with one another. Communication channels need to be organized in a way that takes advantage of each of them so that various aspects of a brand can be conveyed most effectively. In other words, radio may be most effective at making the case for a consumer to choose the brand on the basis of rational benefits, while a television campaign may be more effective in communicating why your brand is better than a competitor's.[10]

This raises the important question of how to communicate your brand to both targeted and nontargeted customers. There is some evidence that targeted customers are more influenced by price and quality, while nontargeted customers are more influenced by price and reputation. This has very important implications in the political marketplace, where candidates are constantly seeking to win over voters who are sitting on the fence and are unsure whom to vote for. To those candidates, issues and policies may be of less importance than the personality of the politician. Let's now explore just how this played out in the 2008 and 2012 Obama campaigns.[11]

The Obama Model

In 2008, Obama went out of his way to run a positive campaign; by comparison, his 2012 campaign was much more negative. Romney was also attacking Obama quite a bit, especially going after Obama's citizenship and past. Obama, on the other hand, attempted to shape the perception that Romney was an untrustworthy leader, focusing on the amount of taxes he paid (or did not pay). Throughout the 2012 campaign, there were some very interesting uses of branding to shape the image of the respective candidates. In a move that mimicked a moment when Hillary had a "shot and a beer" during the 2008 campaign, Obama made it his business to be seen having a Bud Light at the Iowa State fair in 2012, something that Romney would never do because of his Mormon faith. One might raise the question why this tactic was used, and it probably was the result of Obama's attempt to regain the support of young people who had clearly backed him in 2008 but had since cooled toward him because of various stands he had taken during his first term in office.

As we look back at the 2012 campaign, it is clear that Obama struggled to find a brand image that he was comfortable with. The one personality trait that was consistently associated with Obama, both in 2008 and 2012, was that of a political leader who attempted to bring together all factions of the two political parties in an effort to position himself as a leader who was "above the fray," perhaps in imitation of the approach used by Reagan during his two terms in office. This is an effective branding strategy, as long as a candidate can be consistent as he seeks to set himself apart from the competition during the primaries but then move toward the center of the political spectrum during the general election. Jack Pitney, a political science professor at Claremont McKenna College, made the point that a possible reason for the less negative campaign in 2008 was the fact that Obama respected his opponent, John McCain.[12]

From a branding perspective, there are some lessons that stand out from Obama's use of this marketing tool. First, branding is most effective when the targeted audience share their enthusiasm with others, something that certainly took place during the 2012 campaign. In this way, an organization creates ambassadors for its product, giving it the best possible chance of being seen in a positive light by others, including those who may not initially have had a positive view of it. This played out in many ways for the Obama campaign, whether it was through word of mouth between people in a social setting or online interaction in some chat room. Second, it is important to be able to attach a good story to a brand. This played out for Obama at campaign stops and during debates, as well as through all paid media spots that trumpeted his message to followers. For example, in response to the infamous Clint Eastwood speech, where the actor spoke to an empty chair ostensibly meant to represent Obama, the Obama campaign cleverly produced its own version, which wound up playing out all over the Internet. Finally, it always pays to have well-known opinion leaders and celebrities endorsing a product, another strategy the Obama team used very effectively to reinforce the image of the candidate.

Throughout the campaign in 2012, Obama was always on message, with a simple, relevant, consistent theme that was delivered over and over again. This was further reinforced by the personality traits exhibited by the leader – namely, coolness under pressure and openness, as he reached out to others to include them in decision making and give credit to members of the team. Finally, Obama was always careful to criticize Romney's ideas instead of attacking him personally.[13]

What the Obama campaign had going for it in 2008 was its strong brand image and strong message. The slogan "Hope and Change" was very compelling and provided a point for people to rally around. However, with six months to go before the 2012 election, Obama had waited too long to create a unifying slogan. Obama's strategists had tried a few different ones throughout the campaign, but any effort to solidify a brand image would have been looked at as a superficial move. The slogan "An America Built to Last," for example, was used by Obama at some point during the 2012 election cycle and would have been a good slogan for people to get behind, but it could have meant different things to different people. Several other campaign slogans were also considered, including "An Economy Built to Last," "We Can't Wait," and "Winning the Future." The Obama campaign had said that while these slogans were seemingly disparate, they all related to a common theme, which was an economy that was built to last. And even though the Republican primary had not yet been decided, Obama at this juncture in the campaign was running out of time.[14]

The quest for a slogan was much more difficult in 2012 than in 2008 because it had to be based on Obama's accomplishments since taking office in 2008, rather than on promises made when he entered the race during his first term in office as a rather unknown senator without much of a record to fall back on. As the 2012 campaign went forward, the Obama team realized that his greatest achievements were health care reform and the stimulus package, both of which divided public opinion in the country. With the American public most concerned about the economy, Obama's most popular accomplishments (the killing of Osama bin Laden and the ending of the Iraq War) were not the public's biggest concerns.

In 2012, Obama was feverishly searching for a slogan that would allow him to define who he was as a leader and to position himself for the future. When I was interviewed by *Politico* during the time that Obama was searching for a brand identity, I tried to offer an explanation that tied into the work I had done with the Clinton White House, when I helped define Clinton's 1996 re-election campaign with advice that eventually turned into his winning slogan, "A Bridge to the 21st Century."[15] In my comments I said, "He's all over the place." The interview then reported, "a slogan is just a few words for the background of campaign lit and stump speeches. But its importance, Newman explained, shouldn't be understated ... 'That becomes the branding of the whole campaign ...That becomes the anchor to bring together disparate voter segments. It's the glue, if you will.' ... Newman and others agree … [that] the window for Obama to settle on a strong and consistent slogan is closing." (Ronald Reagan's "Morning in America" was locked into place in May 1984, approximately six months before the general election.)[16]

During the 2012 campaign, the Obama team tried to remind the American public about everything that his administration had done since Obama was elected in 2008. This, however, diluted the power of the message. The campaign switched to focus on just a few big issues, and it seemed to be working. Furthermore, focusing on each of these issues every couple of weeks kept Obama in the news, as he was competing for media attention with the candidates running in the Republican primaries around the country. Obama was reluctant to re-adopt his 2008 slogan, "Change We Can Believe In." Instead, the campaign tried to focus on putting out a message that would contrast them with the Republicans, negatively playing off the prior two years during which the GOP was in control, thus trying to associate the negative public opinion toward the government with the Republican Party and, ultimately, the man who would become Obama's opponent, Mitt Romney. When Obama considered using the capture of Osama bin Laden as a tagline for the campaign, it drew a strong response from James Carville, Bill Clinton's strategist in 1992, who said, "I think every instinct is to run on a version of that. Unfortunately, they can't. I don't think the public is with them on that. They're caught between that which they would love to do and that which they can't do."[17] (Eventually it was decided to use "Leadership We Can Believe In," a variation on the 2008 slogan.)

The Role of Image

When Barack Obama threw his hat into the political ring as a virtual unknown in 2007, one of his greatest challenges was to define his image in the minds of voters. Further complicating this task was the need to let voters know that his name, especially his middle name, Hussein, should not inhibit anyone from supporting his candidacy. To effectively carry out this task, Obama relied on the use of branding as a tool to define his image. So, the question that arises is, what is an image? By definition, an image is the perception a citizen holds reflecting what it is that they like and dislike about the politician in question. In the same way in which an image of a product is developed, a political image is influenced by all of the factors that shape how people perceive a politician, including his or her policy stands, personality, character, support by various segments of the electorate and key opinion leaders, and day-to-day reporting in the media about the candidate.

The combination of both positive and negative appeals can shape a politician's image. For example, in 2008, Obama promised to stay above petty politics, by implication suggesting that his opponent, John McCain, was playing by a different set of rules, resorting to tactics below the standard that Obama set for himself. Incumbency is also a factor in shaping a candidate's image. In 2008, being a newcomer allowed Obama to take a negative slant on the economy, while in 2012, he needed to give it a more positive spin.

In 2012, Obama was very effective at shaping *Romney's* image by attacking him and labeling him as someone who could not be trusted, a perception thought by many to be his main weakness as a candidate. However, at the same time, in an effort to shape his image in a more positive light, he referred to Romney's successful career in business, but then raised the question of whether that was sufficient experience for a president.

Branding plays a key role in shaping a positive image of a politician. This ties into the level of consistency that is attributed to the actions of the politician, as well as the use of marketing symbols to portray a particular essence of a politician. (For example, in both his 1980 and his 1984 campaigns, President Reagan was always seen speaking at campaign stops in front of the American flag, a practice that branded him as a loyal citizen and shaped his image as a patriot in the public's mind.) A slogan in a campaign is critical, as in just a few words it becomes the brand of the whole campaign, the glue that brings together and holds together disparate voter segments.

Obama's 2008 campaign came the closest of any presidential campaign in history to resembling an organization managing a brand. It had a slogan that allowed voters to define for themselves the meaning that attached to the candidate and that also resonated consistently across different segments of the electorate. It had one central message and theme, much as the "swoosh" for Nike represents quality to customers who compare it to other brands of gym shoes. In 2012, the Obama consultants' skill in branding helped them not only define the "right" brand for their own candidate but also allowed them to define the opposing candidate's image for him, as they did effectively when they labeled Romney as out-of-touch with the day-to-day struggles of average Americans.[18]

The Role of Consultants in Shaping a Brand Image

Just as companies selling hi-tech products hire consultants to help in their branding and marketing strategies, so all political candidates to-day hire consultants to help define their brand and the image they project.[19] Hiring the right consultants and getting them to work in concert when they all have a different expertise is becoming more complicated. The Obama Model was an example of the successful use of consultants, where experts of all ages and stripes worked together around a table, rather like the team of a start-up company, to bring together a cohesive set of strategic initiatives that allowed them to create a positive and consistent "Obama brand."

Consultants' activities include many different facets of strategy that contribute to the brand of a politician. For example, consultants are necessary to help with day-to-day activities, especially when it comes to a candidate running for office. They help define the promotional strategy, the campaign organization, and the approach to polling and analysis of Big Data sets of voter preferences and past behavior patterns. They also work with various opinion leaders within and outside the party, all of whom contribute significant dollars to a campaign. And of course they provide input into the choice of issues and policies advocated by a politician. The main message here is that these activities do not stop once a candidate wins a race and gets into office, but continue on, subject to different legal restrictions on the use of funds and personnel for different activities, especially for a sitting president in the White House. When it comes to branding and image development, the real challenge to a consultant is to determine exactly what message is coming from all of the research carried out, ascertain the underlying streams of meaning, and then determine the best approach to implement the strategy successfully. This "image management" involves a trade-off between sometimes competing requirements – to respond to citizens' needs, desires, and expectations of their leaders; to portray an image that is consistent with the politician's natural talents and personality; and to constantly respond to attacks by a wide variety of public entities trying to redefine the brand and image a political organization thinks will bring victory during a campaign and success while in office.[20]

The Role of Loyalty in Branding

Consumers are relying less and less on their experiences with a company as the availability of information increases and is easily accessible. At the same time, marketers believe that developing loyalty to a brand is still a profitable approach to maintaining a relationship with their customers.[21] In politics, the same is true; voters can easily ascertain the issue positions and background of new candidates in order to make comparisons when it comes to choosing a well-known versus a less well-known candidate. Recent polls support the idea that American voters are no longer party loyal and have abandoned the proxy criterion of party affiliation: "Forty percent of all registered voters are independents, the highest figure since Gallup started keeping track half a century ago. Since 2008, 2.5 million voters have left the two major parties to become independents, which is now a larger group than registered Republicans or Democrats."[22]

In 2008, the Obama campaign was able to build a brand, slogan, and message that resonated with the American public as a whole. As the Republican Party searched for an image that would both appeal to their base and distance it from the unpopular Bush presidency, the Obama campaign was projecting a unified brand and message. As American consumers (voters) became increasingly inclined to abandon brands they had been loyal to previously when presented with a value proposition that better met their needs, Obama's clear message of "change" implied that it was time to re-examine their loyalties.

In 2008, Obama's brand slogan, "Change We Can Believe In," succeeded as a unifying message that was simple enough to create a mass appeal among loyal Obama supporters yet vague enough to achieve adaptability. "Change" by definition is the very antithesis of loyalty, and the Obama campaign seized the opportunity to profit from consumers' weakened attachments. Further unifying the Obama brand was an acceptance and successful use of social media, mobile applications, and nontraditional media. All of these efforts were an intentional departure from the political status quo and therefore in practice a "change" from what Americans had previously grown accustomed to. In effect, the loyalty that was built up for Obama worked in a similar fashion as it does for companies selling products and services, where the drive to build a relationship with the customer stems from many different points of interaction between the company and the customer.

In the case of Obama, the real lesson to be learned is that loyalty can be built up by creating a "movement" where a single, unifying theme – in this case, change – can effectively be used to rally people together and create a loyal following.

Positioning and Branding

Positioning is a marketing concept that effectively creates a lens with which consumers view a company's entire line of offerings and products. Today's companies spend vast resources to position themselves favorably in the mind of their potential customers. Successful attempts are easy to find in today's marketplace. For example, the Japanese automaker Toyota has done as good a job as any modern company at positioning itself as the maker of a quality, reliable product. This reputation has been earned through years of creating products that meet customers' expectations, and has been cemented by marketing campaigns that highlight empirical evidence that supports it. A successful attempt at positioning a brand and therefore ascribing underlying qualities to its products is essential to brand loyalty. The concept that "you know what you're getting" helps a firm acquire new customers. To use another example from the auto industry, a consumer who has never owned a Mercedes-Benz has a concept of what type of owner experience it provides. Mercedes, through years of positioning itself as a luxury brand with the highest engineering standards, has created a reputation that a single anecdote would be unable to destroy. Potential customers then consider this reputation when they decide to enter the market to purchase a new vehicle.

Today's consumer may be less susceptible to product positioning than in the past, so it was important that Obama was able to adopt a brand identity that was "agile."[23] Obama's brand embraced the changing mindset of the American consumer by remaining flexible and ever-evolving. Therefore, since the brand *was* change, it was able to create a mission, value, and identity without painting itself into an ideological corner. The message was one of inclusion, solutions, and a degree of open-mindedness previously unseen in American presidential campaigns. This message enabled grassroots organizers and fund-raisers to feel like stakeholders in the election bid, thus relying on a positioning strategy that centered on the strength of the brand.[24]

The concept of positioning goes far beyond imagery and recognizable taglines or slogans. While these do go a long way to establishing and measuring the public's recognition of a particular firm or their understanding of a candidate, it is essential to understand the role of positioning in decision making in order to understand the role of political marketing in society. The development of a position and its relationship with a brand is key to winning the support of increasingly uncommitted American voters. A candidate's positioning is often the basis for the average American's choice of a candidate, so understanding how to manage a brand's message can make the difference between success and failure. Further, the message itself (content, imagery, audio) is only one component of the way it is received. An effective marketer understands that the outlet used to promote an idea can sometimes leave a greater impression than the carefully crafted message itself. In business and in politics the intent of a message is irrelevant, while the interpretation of the receiver is the only way by which to measure effectiveness. Therefore, a successful position must present a unified and concise picture of the product, firm, or candidate.

The Use of Social Media Campaigns to Brand Products

Using social media to brand products is certainly becoming much more popular as the world of commerce continues to take advantage of the marketing strength that comes with consumers' endorsements of products to their network of friends. At the same time, many companies have failed in their attempt to brand through social media campaigns by making a few wrong moves. Some well-known mistakes include those by companies such as the Gap and Urban Outfitters, who tied certain promotions to Hurricane Sandy, a move that rubbed people the wrong way. Also, trying to trick users into liking and tweeting alienates more potential customers than it brings in. This is the modern version of extremely gimmicky marketing, and people aren't falling for it. Companies also fail to realize that social media campaigns are not a Monday-to-Friday effort, as everyone has learned by observing the successful use of this technology by the Obama strategists. For example, a company cannot afford to take off a few days. If someone posts something on the Friday of a holiday weekend, it can accumulate a wave of responses over the weekend, while it may be as many as three days before anyone looking at the site even notices. The social media world moves so quickly it can produce unwelcome surprises. At the same time, if their brand takes an unjustified beating on social media, companies should not be afraid to strike back. The company Bodyform hit back at a negative comment with a funny video that went viral. Showing wit during a time of potential conflict really helped them in that instance.[25]

The successful use of social media by the Obama campaigns leaves marketing managers with a strong message, and that is to be careful not to assume that any product or service can rely on the same technology to build up a company's brand. In a Gallup survey of 18,525 adults that was reported in the *Wall Street Journal*, 62 percent said that social media had no influence at all on their purchases; 30 percent said it had some influence; and only 5 percent said it had a great influence. The survey found that 94 percent of the people interviewed said that they use social media to connect with friends and family; 29 percent use it to follow trends and get product reviews; and 20 percent use it to comment on what they do and don't like about products. The conclusion from this Gallup survey is that social media are not currently as useful and powerful as many companies had hoped. This leads one to more carefully inspect why they turned out to be so effective for the Obama campaigns. The answer lies with the use of the technology, which was to activate citizens to get involved in campaign events and to donate funds to support a leader who was also supported by their friends and family. Essentially, the challenge to a for-profit or nonprofit organization is to use the technology to go beyond the reinforcement of the brand, and to encourage the receiver of the information to initiate action via the platform being used.[26]

Purpose-Driven Marketing

"Purpose-driven marketing" is an important concept that continues to influence all branding strategies. One company that follows this model is TOMS Shoes. Since the company was launched in 2006, TOMS has branched out into other markets besides shoes, such as clothing and eyewear, among other products. But beyond the success of the company's expansion into other product categories, it excels at sending out a brand message that transcends its product offerings – presenting itself as well as a charitable firm that reaches out to those in need. The TOMS Shoes policy is to hand out a free pair of shoes to a child in need for every pair that is paid for by a customer. This approach to branding very much ties into the company's desire to be a community-oriented organization that is really in the business of building a movement. The movement includes reaching out to the community and in the process building what TOMS hopes will be a lifelong relationship with its customers. The company spends much of its promotional budget on digital as opposed to traditional media outlets. It may not be a surprise to know that the majority of its customers are millennials who are connecting with the company online through social websites as well as through their mobile devices. Purpose-driven marketing mirrors what the Obama campaigns did to connect with many of their supporters.

Branding in the Nonprofit Sector

Some of the most recognized and trusted brands are nonprofits, such as Habitat for Humanity, Amnesty International, and the World Wildlife Fund. Now smaller nonprofits, such as the Bill and Melinda Gates Foundation and Oxfam International, are taking advantage of branding to grow and set a long-term strategy. However, the existing brand models and language around branding are made in large part for the for-profit sector. In response to this, a framework called the Nonprofit Brand IDEA (brand integrity, brand democracy, brand ethics, and brand affinity) has been created by professors at Harvard University's Hauser Center for Nonprofit Organizations and the Rockefeller Foundation. The creators of the framework interviewed seventy-three nonprofit workers across forty-one organizations and found that common themes throughout the interviews were pride and how a brand can unify an organization. A decade earlier, the leading model for brands was effective communication. The general idea was that if nonprofits could get their name out there, get positive associations with other brands and images, then fund raising would be easier.

Comparison of the use of branding by corporations and nonprofits reveals that nonprofits tend to talk more about their brands with respect to their social goals, internal roles, and communications with various audiences. For-profit branding addresses those issues, too, but perhaps not in the same depth. For nonprofits, good branding helps bring trust, and draws people in. There is, however, skepticism among some nonprofit professionals when it comes to branding. There are four reasons for this skepticism: (1) the association between branding and pursuing profits; (2) a perceived disconnect between overall strategy and brand; (3) a perception of a brand as an incarnation of the leadership's ego rather than as a representation of the organization's needs; and (4) a concern that a strong brand will overpower lesser ones in any collaborations or coalitions, undermining the partnerships. Each of these illustrates different kinds of pride, which is pride in the mission, in planning, in values, and in partnerships.

The Use of Social Media When Branding in the Nonprofit Industry

The U.S. Congress has developed a marketing brand for tourism for the whole country, called Brand USA, to market the country to visitors from around the world. It was established by the Travel Promotion Act to drive the country's first global marketing campaign to promote the United States as a top travel destination and to communicate policies governing protocols for entering and leaving the United States. Brand USA, which was launched in spring 2012, is housed at discoveramerica. com. The logo is interesting because it forgoes any effort to be patriotic, and instead tries to appeal to a wider audience, showing the United States as a welcoming place. This is important, since over the years, the perception has been that the United States has become less welcoming to foreigners. The United States is the world's second most popular tourist destination, but still, Brand USA hopes to attract more visitors from outside North America. The organization's budget of $200 million will help them with that, and they also plan to launch a major social media initiative.[27]

Rebranding Strategies for Nonprofit Organizations

There are several reasons to rebrand. For example, there may be something in your brand (name or logo or slogan) that doesn't show your mission. Or, when someone hears your name, they may not know what your mission is. Often times, nonprofits are in the business of expanding their mission in some way, or are trying to move beyond a local to a regional or national level in their outreach. Any company in the process of rebranding needs to make sure that its programs are consistent with its mission; that the organization is set up to support its programs and mission; that its vision is aligned with its organizational setup; and that its communications and brand clarify its mission.[28]

In general, when it comes to branding strategies, nonprofits need to understand the importance of building a community by focusing on real relationships rather than superficial social media likes or tweets. They need to find ways to personalize the message and appeal to customers' hearts. This can be done by using narratives, pictures, and videos, rather than statistics and charts alone. They also need to establish their organization as a thought leader in their particular area of expertise, using their existing wide base of knowledge to publish meaningful content. Finally, they need to make it easy to receive donations. They should not make people go through multiple layers of logins. As with all branding strategies, they need to keep it simple by gathering supporters' addresses, e-mails, names, and perhaps phone numbers. (A brand for a politician is not much different from a brand for a nonprofit. It must be easily identifiable, perhaps not as immediately identifiable as the Obama brand, but enough to make the interaction with the organization simple.) Finally, nonprofits need to cultivate existing relationships by thanking donors and interacting with them in any way possible.[29]

The branding and rebranding strategies used by the Obama team in moving from the 2008 to the 2012 campaign show an organization following all the tenets put forward in this chapter, a process that allowed the Obama team to take their product, the President, and find the best way to position him and his image to the American people in 2012 as an agent of change. Even though "Leadership We Can Believe In," the slogan in 2012, was not the same as the one used in 2008, "Change We Can Believe In," it did allow the President to position himself to voters as the more attractive alternative in the choice between Obama and Romney.

For-profit corporations often find themselves in a position where they must rely on branding in ways that borrow from both the political and nonprofit worlds. In general, all organizations, whether they are from the political, for-profit, or nonprofit sector, must develop a brand that will gain trust with their targeted customers. This calls for learning everything you can about your target audience. Where do they hang out? What inspires them? What motivates them and shapes their decisions? This information should then be used to establish a meaningful connection between your organization and your customers. If your organization stands for something beyond just a business, people will be drawn to you. Making this happen requires you to get your brand in the public eye as much as you can, in as many different situations as possible. Your organization will need to take time to engage on social media – but remember that just because you have 100,000 followers doesn't mean that they're actually connecting with you. In the end, every brand must stand out from the competition by using a personal, new touch.[30]

Branding Is Essential to All Organizations

Jim Messina, Barack Obama's campaign manager, said that while Big Data was instrumental in Obama's 2012 victory, it was a mix of grassroots door-to-door effort as well as technology that brought the victory. People believed in the message and the vision, and ultimately they bought the brand because they believed in Barack Obama. There are ten conclusions that Messina articulated that all tie into the successful branding of Obama. The conclusions draw on various aspects of marketing and technology, all of which worked together to allow the team to position Obama appropriately as required by the different cycles of the campaign. Perhaps this is the most important conclusion to draw from the use of branding in politics: for any company in any sector in society, there will be public developments and competitive threats that constantly call for a flexible and nimble operation to keep the brand on track and focused. The importance of rebranding is enhanced by the new 24/7 cycle of news and information that permeates all sectors of society and puts pressure on organizations to constantly rethink how the public perceives them. In a political environment, especially a presidential election, the pressure to adapt is intense but for a very brief period; for a profit-oriented or nonprofit organization, the need for flexibility may play out over a far longer period, but is essentially no different from the imperatives of a political scenario. So, here are the considerations that Messina thought were paramount for Obama:[31]

- Public polls skew the results. They rely on landlines due to privacy regulations, and since many young voters and increasing numbers of older voters have only cell phones, the polls skewed the results to favor Romney.
- Hire smart people from different industries, not necessarily with any experience in politics.
- Targeted marketing works way better than mass marketing.
- Spend early. Obama launched attack ads during the summer, and Romney never responded to them, even though Romney had spent a lot more than Obama by the end of the campaign.
- The door-to-door tactics still work, especially in places like Ohio.
- Just because someone is an independent doesn't mean they are a swing voter.
- Pay attention to early voting.
- Without a gripping message, marketing is for nothing.

- Romney wasn't the strongest Republican candidate.
- Obama for America, Obama's 2012 campaign, isn't stopping at the election. It is more of a grassroots movement that will continue on into the future.

Marketers know that the focus needs to be on events that create buzz and social media reactions. Events can include YouTube videos, good blog posts, or even other events such as natural disasters. When an election was only a few months away, Super PACs started dumping money into online advertising, hoping to sway voters in swing states. Politics is spending more and more on social marketing, and Super PACs are the biggest spenders among political groups. Although Obama had more total Facebook followers (many of whom were gained in 2008), ForAmerica, a conservative Super PAC, had more people liking, sharing, and commenting. Some think that the proliferation of ads on television and on the Internet will lead to cynicism among would-be voters and reduce participation in elections. While television ads go out to a broad audience, the beauty of online marketing is that it can target highly specific groups of would-be voters and highlight different aspects of a candidate's brand and image for different groups of voters who are looking for different qualities in a leader. What's even more powerful about online marketing is that voters' friends can endorse certain candidates and causes, which is much more effective than cold calls or house visits. Internet marketing will continue to be highly attractive to all entities that participate in the political process.[32]

If nothing else, branding is a promise or a pact made with a customer, or a voter. A brand should communicate core competencies and convey an expressed commitment to quality. Knowing your positioning and not overextending it is key to a brand. It is also critically important to know who you are in the eyes of your customer and to live up to or exceed that expectation. Do not lose sight of strategy or make decisions that will negatively impact the brand equity that has been created. Consistency is key when growing a brand. This is particularly important in politics, where a politician is constantly being tracked by the media, who will question his or her every move. The added value of a brand is the intrinsic trust developed with the customer base. Decisions that undermine this can take years to recover from.[33]

Defining a brand is key. Being able to draw upon a common phrase or idea can help to keep your brand's identity front-of-mind when making business decisions. By making your mission public and memorable, you've given your customers a standard they will expect and will not hesitate to hold you accountable to. As in politics, a logo must be designed that is recognizable and will stand the test of time. A great logo should be simple enough to be easily recognizable and memorable as distinct and unique. McDonald's golden arches, Coke's trademark script and hue of red, or Apple's bite mark are all excellent examples of logos that fit all the criteria. Once a logo is in place, it must be put everywhere, something that the Obama teams did an excellent job of in both of their campaigns. Ubiquity will create a perception of quality, stability, and popularity. Creating a personality or a narrative that reflects your brand is also very important, especially in politics. Over time, the marketplace will come to associate a certain shade of a color (Coke), a font (Google), a piece of fruit (Apple), or a single letter F (Facebook) with a brand.[34]

Brand strategies for products and services of all kinds are subject to changes in the ways that consumers connect with companies, often through media channels that are beyond the control of the manufacturer. This makes it necessary to redesign tactics to respond to the relationship developed with the customer. This is clearly what the Obama strategists did as they reacted to the challenge of connecting with voters who were getting their information and forming a relationship with the candidate in innovative ways. The new reality in branding comes down to the fact that consumers rely on digital interactions after they have narrowed down their choice set to a few brands, and in many cases rely on social media to make their final choice.

Although marketing has changed dramatically as a result of the advent and widespread use of the Internet, some concepts and principles hold constant: Consumers still expect a clearly developed proposition, which requires that a brand be positioned effectively and that firms develop products that respond to the trends and technological advances in their sector. That is not to say that there cannot be cross-fertilization across sectors, one of the key messages of this book.

With that said, many other aspects have changed. For example, consumers are less likely to use proxy filters like brand when making big-ticket purchases. Today's consumers have an infinite amount of data at their fingertips when considering a purchase. User reviews have replaced word of mouth, giving previously obscure or smaller brands a chance to win orders. Further, the relationship no longer ends once a purchase is made. Now, through social media and reviews, marketers have to monitor what users are saying about their products. This development does offer a chance for firms to create loyalty through in-teraction. As the Internet grows and purchasers are making their decisions more and more on the basis of information with a rational orientation, smaller brands begin to gain loyalty and market share. With such widespread information supplied by other users and free market-ing tools such as social media, consumers are relying less and less on brand names, just as a the voter is relying less on party affiliation as the sole determinant of who a politician is and whether or not to cast a bal-lot for that person.

Chapter Six

Lesson 5: Create a Winning Advertising Strategy

The Obama campaigns used different forms of media in both elections to get out their message, including television, radio, newspapers, magazines, billboards, social media, and the Internet. Each type of outlet had customized messages, targeted to specific segments of voters, some relying on a positive message and image and others using a negative approach. However, of all the hi-tech media outlets used in Obama's campaigns, television was – and still is – the most important medium for getting out a message during a political campaign; it also remains the component in a campaign strategy where the most money is spent, significantly beyond what is spent over social media and through the Internet.[1]

Advertising by definition is a form of communication designed to influence the observer, usually with the intent to move a consumer toward a purchasing decision.[2] The Latin root, *ad vertere*, translates as "to turn toward." In modern times we have come to associate the word "advertisement" or "ad" with the medium in which we encounter these attempts at persuasion. For example, print, television, radio, and billboards are all mass appeals to the public, and many of them are overlooked, dismissed, or ignored. These mass appeals are incapable of discriminating between deaf ears and interested potential consumers. In this chapter, we will explore the techniques used in the 2008 and 2012 presidential elections and critically examine the effectiveness of the candidates' strategies to distinguish between those deaf to their appeals and interested potential voters.

Purposes of Advertising

Marketers use advertising to accomplish three main goals:

1. Build Awareness: The first goal of any marketing communication is to create awareness about a product, service, or general offering. If the end goal of marketing is to increase the likelihood of a sale, it follows logically that awareness is the foundation of a successful marketing mix.

2. Position the product: Once a consumer is aware of a product, a marketer's goal is to attach a positive association to the offering in the mind of the reader. The positioning of the product as an offering that presents an either vague or very specific set of attributes is key to constructing a value proposition. This value proposition is a firm's attempt to differentiate its offerings from those of its competitors in the industry.

3. Establish a brand: Consumer heuristics serve as proxies for research. If a marketer has effectively positioned a company's offerings and delivered on its value proposition then future offerings will benefit from the fulfilled promises of previous products. The consumer, when in the market for another good that serves a different need, will use positive association with previous offerings of a firm to ascribe positive characteristics to its other products. Branding allows marketers a foundation from which they can communicate to consumers.

Ultimately, advertising is nothing more than a tool to build awareness, position a product (or candidate), and establish a brand's identity. In political races, as with the marketing of consumer goods, understanding these three concepts and attempting to address them is meaningless without understanding whether or not the message has been received as intended.[3] Simply put, the only perception that matters is that of your audience. If a product or firm has been successful in the three areas mentioned previously, the fourth purpose of advertising comes into play, which is to maintain awareness. One might think of American cola companies when considering the principal functions of marketing and advertising. One would be hard pressed to find an American consumer unaware of the existence of Coca-Cola, Coke, or Diet Coke. In addition to awareness, most Americans have used the product, know what it tastes like, and have decided whether or not they like it. Coke products have been effectively positioned in the minds of its consumers as sugary beverages of a consistent taste and as staple items to accompany a meal or act as stand-alone thirst-quenchers. One might assume, since Coke drinkers have such a strong baseline awareness of what Coke is and what benefits it delivers, that advertising the brand is just a waste of money. This is a wrong assumption.

What Coca-Cola understands is that its market share will always be under attack. Competitors will always be trying to win orders away from Coke. Coke understands that the most effective way to make sure consumers stay loyal to its brand is to never allow them to forget it exists. This is why Coke, despite being the dominant player in its industry, with the highest market share and some of the most brand-loyal users, must match or exceed its competitors in advertising frequency and spending. The ads themselves do little if anything at all to inform consumers of the value proposition Coke offers; they don't describe the taste or even the effect the beverage will have on the drinker. All these advertisements accomplish is the assertion that Coke is here to stay, and that it is part of American life.

There have been a significant number of articles and books written on the subject of advertising over the years, some of which are considered classics in the field. One of the most prolific authors in this area is David Aaker, whose book in 2013 on brand equity and advertising was devoted to management issues in advertising and sales promotion. Along with this recent book, other classic articles spell out in detail how advertising has changed over time, and how marketing managers need to respond to changes in technology, especially in the area of online advertising. There does remain some skepticism concerning the use of mobile advertising, but according to some researchers, when it is used on a permission basis, there is not as much concern with privacy issues.[4]

The Uniqueness of Political Advertising

The promotion of politicians has taken on new meaning as the Internet continues to play a more important role in all elections. Candidates who seek to define both themselves and their competition have a much expanded arsenal compared to the days of Dwight Eisenhower, when television was the most innovative advertising tool available to politicians. It is no longer possible for a politician to rely on a single media outlet; instead, in part because of a highly fragmented electorate, candidates must mount a coordinated effort that makes use of a cross-media strategy. Political campaigns rely on staff who send out messages via the Internet in an effort to shape and gain access to a wider media net. This may require different tactics to be used for different types of messages. If the message is very negative, it is more effective if it is sent out anonymously by bloggers not associated with the campaign.

For example, during the 2008 presidential campaign, Obama staffers created very strong connections with bloggers who played a prominent role over the Internet. It was a quid-pro-quo, as the Obama camp benefited from getting out a message about McCain that was meant to put a dent in his image, and at the same time, gave the bloggers a role that put them right up there with important interest groups in the Democratic Party, ultimately giving them a sense that to some degree they were a key strategic outlet to disseminate policy information. For the bloggers, there was a pressure to always be on the lookout for new content.[5]

As the campaign moved forward, the advertising goals changed from defining a narrative for Obama to hurting the image of his opponent, John McCain, and at the same time influencing the thinking of key opinion leaders in the media. The 2008 Obama campaign is a good example of an organization that relied on well-developed tactics to affect the thinking of journalists, creating and maintaining strong relationships with them and using those connections to release information on a strategic basis. This brought with it the obligation to give these journalists exclusive rights to critically important news releases.[6]

Within the political world, there is a general consensus that agenda-setting takes place in an effort to connect the content in the media with the interests of the audience. There is evidence that the media are very effective in transferring issue importance to voters. For example, if the receiver of a political message has no interest in the content, the issue will not transfer over to that particular audience, and no agenda-setting will take place.[7] Let's now take a look at the recent Obama campaigns to get a better idea of how these tools were used.

The Obama Model

One of the biggest accomplishments of the Obama team was its ability to let the creative people have a lot of flexibility, allowing them to access the latest information gleaned through their databases, and making it possible for them to test, shoot, and send political commercials overnight. In fact, the integration of "customer relationship management" and "marketing communication strategies" was made possible through the use of one of the biggest databases in the country, built around reams of information on voters. Unlike other organizations in the commercial and nonprofit sectors, where customer relationship management is carried out in a separate venue from communication strategy, usually under the direction of the chief information officer, in the Obama Model, the person in charge was the chief marketing person.

Reliance on real-time data happening in one market at a time was pivotal in making all advertising decisions. A typical corporation might have multiple advertising firms operating at once, making it nearly impossible to integrate the strategy across all agencies. The shared database used by the Obama strategists presents itself as a paradigm shift in this area. Finally, the Obama team relied on a different media mix in different states, depending on the opportunities and capabilities in each market for both traditional and digital formats, and on the targeted segment they wanted to reach.[8]

When a candidate has been selected by his or her party to run for president, it might be hard to argue that building awareness is a necessary step in marketing the candidate. With the 24/7 news cycle, the availability of information via the Internet, and the barrage of stories through social media, it seems it would be nearly impossible to avoid being made aware of a candidate and his or her party affiliation. In addition, the public consumption of news in headline format about where each candidate stands on particular issues is also widespread. Even the parties themselves, in selecting a candidate, have branded the individual in such a way that most can guess where he or she stands on any given issue.

In 2008, the Obama campaign understood that creating awareness of Barack Obama the candidate was not likely to be a challenge they would need to overcome. Likewise, the need to use traditional and expensive television advertisements to announce his candidacy or reaffirm his stance on key issues was debatable. Most political strategists would then have turned to acquisition as the primary objective. After all, what is campaigning if not an attempt to acquire as many voters as possible? Here the Obama team agreed that acquisition was to be the primary objective; however, rather than making acquisition the sole focus of the team, they modified it and included it in a trio of objectives.

The "awareness" the Obama team sought to build was not of the candidate himself but of the need to mobilize supporters. The team understood that by creating active advocates of Barack Obama they could not only increase the size of the electorate, they could be almost certain that each person they added through their network would vote for Obama. Becoming aware of the purpose of a message is as important as the content of the message itself. In politics as in business, cost is always a factor and resources are always finite. One of the areas where the Obama campaign enjoyed its biggest advantage was in the return they saw on the investments made in advertising. One might not consider a brand's social media presence as part of advertising, but if we adhere to the definition introduced in this chapter, it is hard to categorize it as anything else. If the goal of advertising is to "turn consumers' attitudes toward" a product, or in this case a candidate, then a social media presence can be every bit as effective as any traditional ad campaign. In 2012, we saw that perhaps it was Obama's social presence itself that resonated with voters most. It helped to position him as a candidate for today's America and created the value proposition that an Obama White House would be unlike any previous administration.

In 2012, Democrats were able to buy more ads than their Republican counterparts through precise and purposeful targeting. The Obama team, through the use of advanced metrics, was able to target high payoff time slots and programs during which to run their ads. By knowing their target market, they were able to "go to them" where they were already gathering. The Obama team booked time on popular morning radio shows both for advertising and for appearances by the President. Obama staffers also found that they could reach a target demographic by advertising on popular regional radio and television shows.

The Obama team in 2012 used nontraditional media outlets to reach the less "politically inclined" population. During his bid for re-election, between 13 July 2012 and 18 September 2012 Obama was interviewed on many morning shows, Spanish-speaking radio stations, sports radio shows, and urban-aiming radio shows. The content of these interviews was decidedly nonpolitical as he answered questions about pop culture and sports. This reflected the fact that his focus on regionally significant but nationally obscure outlets was a key part of his re-election strategy. Romney, on the other hand, chose to focus on more traditional media, making appearances on national programs, local news broadcasts, and conservative talk radio.

Another key element in the Obama team's advertising strategy was that many of the interviews were discreetly carried out without his opponent becoming aware of them. Obama's team purposely avoided notifying the White House Press Corps about the appearances before they happened; the assumption is that this was intentional, to keep Romney from adopting a response with a similar strategy or attempting to create counter-programming in the region during the President's appearances. The Obama team was intent on reaching audiences by any means whatever, implicitly acknowledging that the election was less a national election than a series of state elections with the goal of reaching a winning margin of electoral votes.

While we are examining the strategies used through the traditional channels of television and radio, it is also important to consider the presence of other organizations in politics. Super PACs are political action committees that are able to accept unlimited and unregulated donations and that often create advertisements in support of the candidate of their choice. In these ads, the Super PAC is able to create its own content and thus influence the national dialogue. Republican Super PACs purchased more ad time and ran more ads than the Democrats, but again, the amount spent may not be a good indicator of performance. In 2012, it may be the case that, although outspent as well as out-advertised, Obama's team was nevertheless better able to control the message being spread. This control likely resulted in a more cohesive message that seemed more deliberate and targeted. Consider these proportions: Of the 215 unique ads produced by Democrats, the Obama campaign produced two-thirds (142) of them directly. On the Republican side, Romney's campaign was responsible for only 36 percent of the ads produced in his support (93 out of 259). The difference in the number of message makers also varied greatly, with twenty-one Democratic outside groups creating ads in support of Obama, while thirty-seven different groups backed Romney.[9]

At the start of the campaign, the Obama team expected to be outspent and decided to formulate a plan to spend "smarter." They focused first by placing ad orders early and thus locking in lower prices. With the early movement, the Obama team invested heavily in defining Mitt Romney before his own campaign was organized enough to create a message to counter Democrats' claims. This technique almost certainly put the Romney campaign on the defensive early on in the process. The timing of these negative ads – broadcast when the airwaves were not yet saturated with political messages – was also important. Had these ads run during typical voter cycles (post-Labor Day), an ad attempting to paint Romney in one light would likely have been followed by an ad of Romney's making. By avoiding this type of juxtaposition, the Obama team knew that their advertisement would be viewed as credible and less likely to be perceived as petty back and forth in the media.

Another key difference in the advertising strategies of the 2012 candidates has been described as "economics versus demographics." The Romney platform was built firmly upon the performance of the economy, and his television advertising reflected that focus. By contrast, the

Obama campaign message focused less on policy and more on getting the attention of targeted segments. The Obama campaign targeted women, Latinos, autoworkers, and young people, and tailored ads to each of these groups. The ads presented Romney as a candidate who didn't represent the interests of each of the specific targeted groups. For example, Obama ads featured women criticizing Romney on abortion, and Latinos and celebrities criticizing Romney in Spanish. A simple count goes a long way to quantifying the approaches of the candidates. Obama and his team created nine unique ads on abortion and thirty-eight in Spanish. Romney messages featured one single ad on abortion and eighteen in Spanish.[10]

The Obama camp outspent Romney in most every television media market. In some states – for example, Florida – Obama spent as much as 50 percent more than the Romney camp. In Ohio, Iowa, and other battleground states, it was a similar story, but not necessarily as great as 50 percent. This ran contrary to the thinking at the beginning of the campaign, when most pundits thought that the Super PACs supporting Romney would outspend Obama. In addition to spending more on broadcast television, Obama also spent large amounts on cable, nearly twice the number of channels that Romney used. Interestingly enough, Obama targeted women by putting his commercials on shows like *The View* and soap operas, and then targeted younger voters by putting commercials on *Late Night with Jimmy Fallon*. Romney, on the other hand, attempted to win over male voters by spending on ESPN and BET, where he tried to appeal to African-American men. Another difference lay with the organizational structure of the media-buying team in both camps. Obama used a large firm outside the campaign that had several people working, while Romney relied on an in-house operation that was directed by one person.[11]

Some of the noteworthy statistics are that Obama out-fundraised Romney ($1.2 billion versus $1.18 billion) and outspent Romney ($1.11 billion versus $928 million). Romney raised more from the RNC than Obama did from the DNC ($351 million versus $298 million), and also raised more than Obama from Super PACs ($225 million versus $92 million). Obama raised more from individuals ($733 million versus $479 million). For both there were also significant donations of undisclosed amounts from undisclosed sources.[12]

Throughout the campaign, the Obama camp understood that choosing the correct outlets was critical to their success in reaching those voters less inclined to be interested in the campaign, which meant they had to rely on nontraditional outlets. According to one media expert, James Winston, the executive director of the National Association of Black Owned Broadcasters, "What the president is doing with his outreach to the black community is what every successful candidate knows he must do – black radio is the way to go. If I'm an African American, I can listen to something on the radio and it is talking to me personally. It is the way to engage the African American community." In an effort to compete with Obama to reach some targeted audiences, Romney appeared with his wife on ACC's *Live with Kelly and Michael*. In effect, Obama's advertising strategy was carried out on a state-by-state basis, with the intention of moving toward the goal of 270 electoral votes to win the White House.[13]

In the final days before the polls closed, Obama and Romney planned their last campaign stops. Obama held larger rallies than he had earlier in the 2012 campaign, but the larger rallies were still far smaller than some of his massive 50,000-person 2008 rallies. Both Obama's and Romney's senior advisors and campaigners traveled with them. It seemed that both candidates' focus was on discrediting the other as the final appeals were made. Obama used radio ads to target black voters. One message used a male announcer rallying the demographic around Obama's election success in 2008 and urging the audience to "stick together." Ninety-five percent of black voters cast ballots for Obama (black voters made up 13 percent of the total electorate). The Obama campaign bought ad space attached to search terms such as "Obama singing," "Obama birthday," "Warren Buffett," and "Obama Bracket," thinking that people who search for these would be potential Obama voters. Similarly, Romney purchased ad space attached to search terms "Rush Limbaugh" and Romney's father's name.[14]

The Obama campaign in 2012 teaches some tactical lessons. First, it is important for the advertising campaign to begin very early in the election cycle. For example, even before Romney declared his candidacy, the strategists directing Obama's campaign were already on the air in some swing states, branding Romney's image with selected segments of voters. This is a lesson not to be taken lightly by corporations that are planning a "roll out" of a product, especially one where there is a great deal of competition. It is also important to note that the Obama strategists carried out this campaign on both traditional as well as digital media.[15]

Emerging Technological Advances in Advertising

Micro-targeted ads are replacing the "traditional" Internet advertisements that used to be purchased based on the demographics of people who visited a page. A short time ago, marketers wanting to appeal to potential car buyers would have purchased ad space on popular car magazines' websites or attached their ads to text that appeared within the site. Now, users themselves are telling their browser which ads to show them, regardless of what page they are intending to visit. The Obama team recognized this and more than quintupled their Internet spending from 2008 to 2012.[16]

Just as digital advertising was a key component in the advertising arsenal of the Obama campaign, it is also becoming part of all organizations' advertising strategy. Digital advertising allows companies to control who sees their ads and allows them to create a more interactive environment between sender and receiver, making it a very attractive alternative for corporations. This outlet also offers companies the ability to communicate with their customers at any time, without the restrictions that come with more traditional advertising outlets. In 2012, nearly all global regions saw a rise in digital ad spending. The *New York Times* Company's net income tripled in the last quarter of 2012, in large part because of digital ad sales. Digital advertising is very attractive to marketers because they can more carefully target their audiences, measure the impact of their ads, and create a more interactive environment in which to operate.[17]

These advances in advertising have led to some drastic changes for more traditional outlets, moving this business community into the lap of experts who understand the digital revolution that has taken place. For example, the decline in newsstand sales and subscriptions has prompted Time Warner to consider selling many of the magazine titles in its publishing division to Meredith Corporation, a publishing house with many successful niche magazines. (Time Warner is keeping its bigger magazines, such as *Time, Sports Illustrated,* and *Fortune.*) In these difficult times for traditional publishers, it's important to focus on both digital and print versions.[18] Organizations in all sectors of society are affected by this evolution.

There is movement to the use of the mobile phone as an advertising outlet, a trend that must be considered as CEOs consider how best to implement their advertising strategy. For example, according to Citrix, an American multinational software company that sells software and other hi-tech services, over the twelve months from February 2013 to January 2014, mobile advertisement audiences grew by 100 percent. Approximately 5 percent of tablet and mobile advertisements are now in video form. Fifty-nine percent of the consumers in a survey were under the impression that mobile ads did not count against their wireless plan's data allowance, but they in fact do. Apps continue to be developed in two formats, one a free version supported by ads and another an ad-free premium app that usually costs a nominal fee to download or might require a monthly subscription fee.[19]

As mobile devices become the absolute "remote control" of consumers' lives, marketers must find ways to continually engage them. Today's mobile consumer is perpetually in the considering stage and just a tap away from leaving a physical space and moving to a virtual space. Also, as social media advertising becomes a "pay to play" landscape, marketers are becoming increasingly willing to pay to have their ads highlighted or promoted. Original content that can be accessed across all platforms and devices will continue to be very influential. Mobile devices will be the platform of the future.[20]

Emerging Trends in Advertising: Some Old and Some New

The elections of 2008 and 2012 were heavily influenced by the Obama campaign's ability to define itself through effective messaging, managing the brand it had created, and even defining the message about the opposing candidate at an early stage. Through effective advertising purchases, the Democrats were able to position not only the President but also his opponents. By having a clear and concise strategy, they were able to manage the message effectively even when they weren't creating the content. The Obama team didn't just target key members of the electorate, they also targeted channels and programming. They abandoned, at times, the large net approach of advertising on network television and instead zeroed in on individuals through text messages and well-placed ads linked to browsing history. They didn't just put advertisements where their target demographics were likely to see them, but also tailored those advertisements to the demographic. By appealing to voters and clearly soliciting actions from them, the 2012 Obama campaign created a message that was agile and robust enough to withstand any offensive mounted by its opponents while enlisting supporters to join the cause. Much like Coke, the Obama campaign was able to take advantage of the brand it had created in 2008, and was therefore able to plan counter-strategies well in advance. In a way, through effective and consistent messaging, the Obama brand had obtained loyalty from its 2008 efforts.

There are several trends emerging in advertising that will have a profound impact on the choice of effective advertising strategies. One emerging trend is location-specific advertising. As devices become more interconnected and more prevalent, consumers will be micro-targeted more and more. Personalized data on habits, patterns of consumption, and location will allow advertisers to personalize ads based on up-to-the minute information. This is an area that the Obama team took advantage of, especially in the 2012 campaign. Cognitive computing is also on the horizon, in which machines will be able to learn, infer, and in some ways think, thus making predictive advertising possible. As the desire on the part of marketers in all industries is to seek out real-time impressions and chances to interact with consumers, there will be more viral content like videos and images in outlets such as social media, messaging apps, and image-sharing sites like Instagram. This also brings into the equation the notion that companies will have to rely on consumers as marketing partners rather than targets. Along with this movement will be a new wave of privacy-conscious consumers, being catered to by some of the newer apps like Snapchat, which intentionally does not store information.[21]

Despite these technological advances in the advertising world, television advertising is still leading in overall advertising dollars spent, although it is growing at a much slower rate than digital. While advertising agencies have typically focused on traditional media like print, radio, and television, the industry is becoming increasingly digital. Even stationary advertisements such as billboards and posters are being replaced by digital technologies. There will continue to be a consolidation of agencies, with larger agencies holding negotiating power and achieving economies of scale. Creativity and methodology will be more important as consumers move farther away from traditional media. Data will continue to influence the space as micro-targeting becomes more prevalent, and customer feedback will continue to shape the future of marketing. With real-time results available, agile marketers who can deftly adjust their approach will have the most success in carving out their niche and will remain ahead of the learning curve. This is where the Obama team excelled in the implementation of its advertising campaign, especially in 2012.[22]

Advertising is certainly going to evolve even further in the future, and in unpredictable ways. Such innovations notwithstanding, however, in the end the candidate who is best able to be ahead of the trend is most likely to experience success. As devices continue to rely on connectivity, the ability to model ideal consumers will surely have a large impact on the future of marketing. If there is one lesson to take from the presidential elections of 2008 and 2012, and the Obama Model described in this book, it is that consumers are responding increasingly to value propositions created for the individual, and when faced with a choice between tailored offerings and those meant to appeal to a large population, segments are choosing the former in increasingly significant proportions.[23]

Chapter Seven

Lesson 6: Build a Relationship with Your Customers

The past ten years have changed the way customers interact with the brands and companies they patronize. Through the proliferation of mobile devices and their ability to access social media, more consumers have become "vocal" and now willingly offer critiques and commentary regarding almost any interaction they have with a firm. As a result, brands and companies have to learn to make use of interactions with and feedback from their customers in order to find new and effective ways to grow.

Social media have become key elements in the toolkit of all organizations in their effort to maintain a relationship with their customers. In a classic article on this subject, Andreas Kaplan and Michael Haenlein define the term and distinguish social media from related technologies such as Web 2.0 and User Generated Content. They make the point that while Web 2.0 is a collaborative digital platform, the term "social media" represents a group of applications that are built on ideological and technological foundations that foster the exchange of content between users. Further, they go into a detailed discussion of the different types of platforms that are used, including collaborative projects, blogs, content communities, and social networking sites, among others. They also make extensive recommendations for when an organization decides to use social media, such as the importance of choosing the right form of social media based on the target audience; ensuring that there is the proper alignment across various social media platforms; integrating the content with the brand of the organization; and finally, providing employees with the opportunity to use social media platforms at work.[1]

Other scholars in this area have devoted their attention to the different methods of social media marketing that managers can use to align a user's conversation with the brand of an organization. There is the possibility that social media can take control away from managers and give it to customers. In an effort to deal with this reality, the recommendations to a manager are to start talking to customers instead of trying to control the conversation. Managers need to use new tactics to create a meaningful conversation with the customer and establish a new structure for their integrated marketing communication strategy, which is the attempt to coordinate the various elements of the promotional mix to deliver a more unified message to the customer. Social media, or what some have referred to as consumer-generated media, offer organizations a new variety of online sources that can be used by customers who seek to educate themselves and their friends about different products.[2]

The field of relationship marketing has grown significantly over the past few decades. The term "relationship marketing" was first introduced by Leonard Berry in an edited book he published in 1983, followed shortly afterward by Barbara Jackson in her book on this subject in 1985. One of the best reviews of the literature can be found in Robert Palmatier and colleagues (2006) and in Raji Srinivasas and Christine Moorman in 2005. Each of these articles puts forward the theoretical background in this area, and points out in detail the factors that influence the effectiveness of following a strategic orientation based on this approach. In an influential article in 2004, Evert Gummesson discussed the importance of the value of the relationship between a company and its customers, making the point that the long-term view is what counts in business. The research in this field points to the way in which a customer identifies with a company, and the significance of using direct communication as the company seeks to maintain that relationship. Certainly the development of the social media field has played a very important role in this area.[3]

Consider the sales funnel, where a consumer in the market for a product first becomes aware of a product or brand; then a company becomes aware of a customer's interest, which becomes a "lead." At this point the company tailors a value proposition for the prospective customer; and assuming the offer is sufficiently attractive, the hope is that the prospect may be converted to a sale. In the digital world of e-commerce and social media, customers can move through the sales funnel and make a purchase decision before a firm knows they are in the market. This has led to an attempt on nearly every website that sells anything or even advertises to capture a method of contacting a browser. Without these "leads," a buyer may make a decision before the company has a chance to make contact and offer the customer a value proposition.

To be effective, marketers have to be aware of the bombardment of options and propositions American consumers are faced with on a daily basis through advertisements, e-mail marketing, and even the U.S. Mail. Savvy marketers will use the ever-increasing amount of data available both to tailor their value propositions to customer profiles and to time them to coincide with a likely buying period. Again, this does not complete the sale. Even if a proposition represents considerable value and is timed properly, it must be delivered through the correct medium and reflect a voice that the target identifies with. To put it simply, not just *what* and *how* but also *who* all matter. In today's market, segments are shrinking. The opportunity to understand the decision-making behavior of individuals is the key to refining offerings. Firms today need to understand that capitalizing on opportunities to interact with consumers on their terms is the most crucial element to building brand loyalty.[4]

Consumers and Voters Now Have a Voice

In an age in which we're interconnected with our entire social circle through our fingertips, negative word of mouth and/or negative press have become real concerns of brand managers. The idea that a customer's bad experience might be repeatedly communicated to family and friends over time is a well-accepted truth among developers of customer service strategies. The damage that can be done by a single customer depends on the number of people that customer shares the experience with. While some firms rely on word of mouth exclusively to grow their customer base, most attempt to position and market their brand so that the risk of losing a potential customer due to bad word of mouth is mitigated by a pre-conceived notion of the brand or firm.

In the age of digital social media, an experience that could have previously warranted a letter to a business owner, a few unkind words shared among friends and family, and perhaps the loss of a single customer can now cost a firm in perpetuity. Sites like Yelp.com have not only given consumers a chance to voice their displeasure but have also created a place where the experience itself can reside indefinitely. Rather than relying on advertising or first-hand experience, today's consumer is likely to turn to public opinion when determining whether or not to make a purchase or visit a new restaurant. Even e-commerce sites have adopted the principles of the approach. For online shoppers, included with the description of a product and any technical details are reviews by others who have purchased the item. In short, the dialogue between consumers is increasingly beyond the control of brand managers, however hard they may try to influence the conversation.

The Effectiveness of the Internet in Politics

There continues to be a debate on the relationship between political success and the use of the Internet, with those researchers who document it drawing on the relationship between social media activity and engagement in political activities. In one study carried out in this area, when two U.S. Congressional election cycles were used to analyze a random sample of over 3 billion tweets to generate a usable sample of more than 540,000 political tweets across approximately 800 contested elections, a significant relationship was found between tweet share and vote share. The importance of this finding lends credibility to the use of this medium in both of Obama's election victories, particularly in 2008. Whereas Obama's opponent in 2008, John McCain, was a much more experienced politician than Mitt Romney in 2012, McCain's campaign strategy proved to be outdated when faced with the social media expertise used in the Obama campaign.[5]

Other researchers have found that in 2012 the Romney and the Obama campaign Facebook pages used very similar tactics. As happens in politics at the presidential level, candidates in successive election cycles tend to learn from the mistakes of their predecessors. This was the case in 1992 when Clinton decided to respond to any attack on him or his policies immediately, in order to avoid the mistake that Dukakis made in 1988 when Bush attacked him consistently without any rebukes. In 2012, Romney faced a similar situation, realizing that McCain in 2008 had never moved his social media campaign to a level that was competitive with Obama. In light of the failings of McCain on social media, Romney used the tactics of the Obama campaign and was much more progressive on the social media front. Research on this subject also reveals that Facebook has been a very effective fund-raising tool when it is used to stay in touch with followers.[6]

With the movement toward online participation in all political campaigns, there is evidence to support the fact that political participation increased in the 2012 presidential campaign as a result of the increase in attention paid to the campaign websites. In fact, it was determined that 36 percent of adults in 2012 used the Internet to find information on the campaign, and 17 percent indicated that social media were used as a source. Furthermore, there was a high correlation between the political participation of young people between the ages of eighteen and twenty-nine and their voting activity. In fact, this segment of voters used social networks to promote political material and encourage their friends to vote. However, besides the fact that social media proved to be effective in motivating young people to get involved in politics, research indicates that when it comes to influencing voter turnout, voters who relied on the more traditional media outlets, and in particular television, were more likely to cast a ballot on election day.[7]

The Obama Model

Research carried out on the 2012 campaign that looked at the Facebook timeline photographs of both Romney and Obama revealed significant differences in the way the candidates used the site. First of all, voters already knew what the President "should" look like, as Obama was all over the news all of the time, either hosting other heads of state or addressing various groups of citizens at a range of functions. However, Romney's challenge was slightly different, as he was not as well known as Obama and therefore had to work harder to create an image in voters' minds that matched the image he was trying to portray. It should therefore not be surprising to know that Romney posted nearly twice as many photo statuses as Obama in his attempt to make himself as familiar as Obama. In effect, in an effort to build up his credibility with voters, Romney used patriotic images of himself, such as pictures showing him interacting with war veterans. This relationship-building effort equates with another topic that was addressed earlier in the book, namely branding.[8]

Obama was very effective at building positive relationships with his constituency in both of his campaigns, relying on channels appropriate to the demographic characteristics of the selected voter group. For example, he was able to rely on social media to connect with young women, Hispanics, African-Americans, and Asian-Americans. Different groups access information in different ways. For example, Hispanics use mobile and social media more than their white counterparts. Whites also lag behind other groups in adoption of Twitter. In 2008, Obama dominated social media, much as he did in 2012, but in 2008, it was a totally different, simpler game. Obama's messages in 2012 were much different than Romney's, focusing more on building communities online. A lot of the activity, such as e-mails, would serve to do tasks such as remind people to vote, rather than try to change people's minds.[9]

During the 2008 campaign, Barack Obama's website had a different version for each state (e.g., oh.barackobama.com was Obama's Ohio website), and the website provided a significant amount of information on Barack, Michelle Obama, and Joe Biden. There was also a blog that was meant to reveal their personalities. There was a Spanish version, and also ones that focused on special groups such as military families, people with disabilities, and even Republicans. The website also gave fans of the website opportunities to campaign for Obama – for example, by showing a map of the fan's neighborhood where they'd like to spread the campaign effort and providing instructions on such things as how to hold a debate party. The Obama campaign also devoted a lot of money and attention to paid advertising (e.g., using Google Adwords) and online display advertising. An example of this in use was determining a topic that might be used in one of the debates. The campaign also used in-video game advertising with certain Xbox Live titles. All of these outlets were avenues to build relationships with different segments of voters.[10]

The Obama team understood the importance of interacting with the receiver of a message, and put initiatives into play that engaged the public. While understanding communication channels is key to any politician's bid for office, the campaign's mastery of these techniques was the deciding factor in making Barack Obama the President of the United States. The Internet as well as mobile applications were the game-changer for Obama in much the same way as radio was for Franklin Delano Roosevelt and television was for John Fitzgerald Kennedy.[11]

In the marketing literature, it is an axiom that consumers who are more engaged on any level with an organization are more likely to feel connected to it, and hence to solidify their relationship through a given activity. One such activity is the donation of funds to an organization, regardless of the amount given. Once the person goes through the act of giving, it serves as a sort of glue that makes reaching out to that same person in the future that much easier and more effective for the organization. Fund raising is a major component in the campaign process, and the Obama team in 2012 used some surprising tactics based on their data about potential campaign contributors. Jim Messina, the Obama campaign manager, was quoted as saying that the team would "measure every single thing." He followed this statement up by quin-tupling the size of the 2008 analytics team, pulling in experts from business as well as politics. (In fact, the Obama team's "chief scientist" had gained notoriety by using data to design more effective super-market promotions.)[12]

The Obama team used e-mail incredibly effectively, bringing in more donations through e-mail than from any other Internet source. By the end of the election, they had 13 million e-mail addresses. Over 100 dif-ferent versions of e-mail messages were sent out, with demographics, geography, and other features determining who got which e-mail. Every aspect of the e-mails was tested, from e-mail subject lines to content, to find the most successful combinations that would result in high rates of opening. Each e-mail also had a very clear "call to action," asking read-ers to share information or make donations.

During the course of the 2012 campaign, social media helped Obama raise $147 million from small donors who donated less than $200; by comparison, Romney raised only $39.5 million from small donors.[13] By the 2012 campaign, Twitter was more influential than it had been in 2008. Tumblr was used primarily by the younger audience. Facebook remained a huge player, and is still probably the best way, apart from television and radio, to reach large numbers of people. YouTube was used by both candidates to show videos, including some that were shown on TV. Although Instagram, Pinterest, and Spotify didn't have as many followers in comparison with Twitter and Facebook, they were all effective because they brought out the personality of the user.[14]

Almost 70 percent of voters under twenty-five (often labeled "the Facebook Generation") voted for Obama. Obama was the first presi-dent to get that high a percentage from that demographic since exit polling started in the 1970s. Facebook played a large role, encouraging online debates about issues. Facebook also partnered with ABC for election coverage, while CNN partnered with YouTube for the presi-dential debates. The 2008 election marked a huge shift from traditional old-style politics toward social media networks. Through the Internet, grassroots support could gather together in communities. Another im-portant feature of social networks is that there are no barriers to entry, so everyone can participate.[15]

The Pew Research Center's Project for Excellence in Journalism came out with a study about Obama's and Romney's websites and their post-ings on Facebook, Twitter, and YouTube. Some highlights of the find-ings were as follows:

- Obama posted four times more content online than Romney did, was active on twice the number of social platforms, and had his content shared more than twice as often as Romney. On Twitter, Obama averaged twenty-nine tweets per day, as compared to Romney's one per day. Obama posted two times more blog posts and more than two times more videos on YouTube.
- Both candidates posted more messages about the economy than about other topics, but according to sharing statistics, the majority of users found immigration, women's rights, and veterans' issues to be more important.
- Social networks are set up to have a two-way conversation with voters, but both Obama and Romney tended to use communication only in a one-way broadcast style. The only place where Obama let citizens' voices be heard was on his blog, where the content could be controlled. About 33 percent of Romney's content was about Obama, whereas Obama talked about Romney only 14 percent of the time. In July before the election, however, Obama's content did increase its references to Romney.
- Obama's website allowed visitors to join groups such as African-Americans, women, or LGBT voters, which shaped the type of content those followers received. Romney's website did not offer this at all.

The question that is being raised by many is whether such social media activity translates into votes. Obama won the 2008 election largely because of young voters. Did those young voters vote for Obama because of his message and what he stood for, or did they vote for him because of his social media activity? Or was it some combination of the two? It's hard to actually say. In general, successful presidential candidates have adapted to changing communication trends. John F. Kennedy embraced television, and Obama was the first to harness social media.[16]

In 2008, Obama had 5 million supporters across fifteen different social networks, including BlackPlanet, a MySpace-type site for African-Americans, and Eons, a Facebook for baby boomers. He had 3.2 million Facebook followers, and Facebookers could add a button to their profiles that said "I Voted." Joe Rospars, the director of Obama's new media department, had a staff of thirteen devoted to Internet marketing throughout the primaries, which was significantly more than McCain or Hillary Clinton had. As the election progressed, Rospars had upwards of thirty people reporting to him. He used paid advertising to drive everyone to BarackObama.com. If you were a fan of Obama's Facebook page, you would see the advertisements just about every time you went online. There was also an analytics team that measured all of the information that took users to BarackObama.com. They tested to see which ads got the most people to the page, and which e-mails were opened the most.[17]

Important Differences between 2008 and 2012

In assessing the successes and failures of the 2008 campaign, the Obama team determined that there were far too many databases in play. The team kept separate files by region for volunteers and contributors. In 2012, the team used a single database that was accessible by campaign staffers through a single "dashboard" application. The new consolidated database allowed campaign marketers to model appeals for specific voters. The team focused on what they viewed as key demographics, segmented by age, race, gender, and voting record, and then applied "persuadability" metrics using consumer data. From these data, the team were able to identify people who were most likely to give online or who were most likely to volunteer. By modeling voters, the team were able to focus their efforts on those most likely to respond positively, making the team much more efficient than in 2008.[18]

Below are some of the key differences among the social platforms:[19]

1. Facebook: Facebook had only 100 million users in 2008; in 2012 it had 1 billion users, reflective of the global reach of this platform. Since 2008, Facebook has also launched the "like" button, Facebook connect, where people can log on to other sites using their Facebook credentials, as well as expanding the length of their posts.
2. Twitter: It was only about two years old when the 2008 election took place. In 2012, it was such a huge part of media and elections that there really is no comparison between the two election cycles. Obama tweeted minutes after his re-election, and that picture of him and Michelle Obama is now the most re-tweeted tweet of all time. Twitter now has more than a billion tweets every two days.
3. Instagram: It did not exist in 2008, but it became an important platform in the 2012 election as an all-visual medium.
4. Foursquare: It did not exist in 2008. Geolocation services are going to become more important in the future.

5. Pinterest: It did not exist in 2008, and now the design-focused site has more than 25 million monthly visitors.
6. Tumblr: It did exist in 2008, but it did not have an impact on the election. In 2012, it became an important social media site, especially for younger voters.
7. Mobile: The iPhone came out in June 2007, but it really hadn't reached the volume of people it has by now. In the 2008 election, SMS messages were being sent out. In 2012, consumption of mobile content skyrocketed and will only keep increasing.
8. The World Wide Web: The web is no longer the main space, given all of the social networks and electronic devices available, but it continues to maintain an important role for all organizations, as most graphic content still is created and first dispersed over the web.

Making the Leap to Commerce

In the early days of social media, there was a simple way for businesses to engage in two-way dialogues with customers and other people. However, once marketers began to apply their understanding of technology to these platforms, relationships were cheapened, taking on more of a transactional focus rather than centering on engagement and the building of rapport. There is now a movement toward having marketing departments take over the control of social media. For example, in organizations, social media used to be separate from the hierarchical structure of a company. Now social media are under the marketing wing. Companies are trying hard to measure return on investment (ROI) of something that is clearly beneficial yet at the same time hard to measure. Also, while the focus of social media used to be on listening to and understanding the individual, now it is increasingly becoming like corporate broadcasting, where individuals are no longer valued.

It is important therefore not to mistake social marketing for interaction with real people. There is marketing behind it, and that means a sales-oriented vocabulary and mentality, so one needs to be careful. While social media have indeed changed, that is not to say that they shouldn't be used for marketing purposes. They still offer very effective ways to create buzz and awareness about products and events. Going forward, those who engage with and truly listen to their customers and understand their needs will be successful. Ultimately, listening closely to your customers makes it possible to build long-term relationships with them.[20]

Building Relationships in the Nonprofit Sector

Social media can be tapped to raise money in many different sectors in society. It can be as easy as installing a Facebook program called "Causes" that lets people donate directly to your cause. Nonprofits are also having great success using the efforts of their supporters on social networking sites such as Twitter and Facebook to rally people for live fund-raising events or just to collect donations. The Water Society and the Humane Society of the United States are two organizations that are successful in using social media to get people to donate. According to a study by the Center for Marketing Research at the University of Massachusetts Dartmouth, eight out of ten charities said they use social networking, and nine out of ten said their efforts were successful, both increases from the year before. Running mass social media campaigns to get donations isn't for every organization, though. They can be time- and labor-intensive. What's more, social media don't provide a guaranteed route to fund-raising success. While social networking might not be the best means of fund raising, it is definitely important for building a community that cares. Having a loyal following with a deep connection to the organization is essential and can bring great long-term success to organizations.

Another good thing about social networking is that it puts social pressure on friends of those involved. That was the idea behind the Charities Facebook app. This easy giving also lets people get off the hook by donating a little, and then feeling good, without actually getting involved with the organization. This is known to critics as "slacktivism." A further criticism is that while a certain charity or nonprofit might have thousands of "likes," the number who actually interact deeply with the cause or the organization may be much smaller. The big question with social networking and nonprofits is how an organization measures the return on investment. Typically, charities and nonprofits measure success and engagement in terms of hours or money donated. For example, on Facebook, it's hard to measure a "like." Can you track who sees it and how those people are influenced by the social pressure of knowing one of their friends is supporting a cause? Being able to do this will become very important going forward.[21]

The Diabetes Hands Foundation launched the Big Blue Test campaign, urging people to test their blood glucose and post pictures of the readings on Twitter or Instagram. Then participants were told to exercise and take new pictures to show the lower blood glucose count. Malaria No More got well-known comedians to do funny videos that raised malaria awareness via social media platforms. They called the campaign "malarious." Finally, Stand Up to Cancer used stand-up comedians for entertainment as they broadcast their fund-raising telethon live on TV, but also on Hulu, which garnered lots of attention. Each of these nonprofit companies was successful in building relationships through social media.[22]

The March of Dimes raised awareness of a memorial service online and engaged with supporters and donors. Community members rallied around this networked cause and organized the memorial service themselves – without the March of Dimes organization having to do anything. Social media make it easier and easier for individuals to support causes. Just throw up a Facebook page around a cause and people can join up and organize fundraisers. The Facebook Causes Birthday app uses people's birthdays online as a "hook" to get donations toward certain causes. This does make it easier for nonprofits to find groups that already exist around their particular cause and to engage those groups with a minimum of effort. Many organizations now use crowd sourcing to solicit ideas, get feedback, and collaborate with their community members online. Some successful groups that have done this are WeAreMedia, with a wiki project that crowd-sourced best practices for social media use, and YouTube Symphony Orchestra, with the winners of a performance contest being voted in via YouTube. The National Wild Life Federation and the American Red Cross have also had great success with such culture change endeavors.[23]

Building Relationships Is the Future

The Obama campaigns of 2008 and 2012 relied on social media to build stronger relationships with many different constituencies. The result of this process leaves us with some general lessons that can be applied to organizations in other sectors of society. Always focus on individuals. A major goal of the social media campaign was to build relationships by focusing on people connecting with Barack Obama as a person. This attracted many people to vote for him, since he wasn't just some unknown politician. Part of the campaign team's effort also focused on authenticity. For example, Obama's Facebook page made reference to his favorite sports and his favorite movies, and had pictures of him and his kids. Obama's staff would post "real" content as well, such as how they were taking a break to get pizza. Fully 80 percent of the $639 million Obama raised was from donations of $20 or less. The Obama campaign hosted a few dinners to which donors – of any amount – were invited, subject of course to winning a lottery. This made such events – which are typically only for the elite of major donors – much more democratic. The dinners were also posted and streamed live on YouTube. The campaign also did several successful tactical things such as allowing followers to create their own Barack Obama pages and efforts; having a call to action with every e-mail and every communication; having a clear vision and message; and continually networking and building relationships with everyone.[24]

While the Obama campaign may have secured two elections with a savvy media strategy, one may also argue that they didn't face much opposition in building relationships with voters by securing the Internet advantage. In future elections this most likely will not be the case. The Obama team's success is sure to provide a best-practices benchmark that both Democrats and Republicans would be foolish not to emulate and expand on. The same can be said for firms looking to gain a competitive advantage, as increasing numbers of firms try to assert their presence through social media.

While nonprofit companies are also using social media, they continue to make tactical mistakes. They spread themselves too thin by joining Facebook, Twitter, Pinterest, Instagram, and a host of other networks. In the beginning, it might be easier to engage with supporters on just one of these platforms, before expanding to others. When nonprofits do too much, the brand tends to be diluted, and both audience engagement and content suffer. This means that organizations must engage with every follower on social media. In the beginning, nonprofits should also engage with every commenter and re-tweeter, thanking them for their support and using the forum to build deeper relationships. By doing this, they will create value by giving their supporters content they'll actually care about. It is mandatory that organizations don't just post for the sake of posting; each piece of information published should offer solutions, build relationships, or gain respect.[25]

Some recent trends in this area include the elimination of surveys. According to Kristin Muhlner, CEO of NewBrand Analytics, surveys are a less efficient way of gathering the opinions of customers. Social feedback is open forum, honest, and unbiased. Industrial espionage can now be legal and free. Simply use competitors' social feedback to get a better handle on issues of concern to them. By using the feedback of users of an industry's leading firm, you'll be able to improve your offerings in a way that can help win orders and market share. If your company has a storefront, chances are someone has written about his or her experience there. Using this to evaluate employees will ensure they're always acting as if they're "on stage." By using sites like Yelp and customer reviews, a multi-unit company can very easily monitor the reputation and satisfaction of its customers from all over. If underlying sales data tend to corroborate a problem, social media can allow management to act on a problem before it becomes too late. Finally, as mergers and acquisitions become more and more prevalent, regional businesses are increasingly entering new markets. As a consequence, a bad experience reported by a customer in Chicago may be communicated to your firm's customers in San Francisco.[26]

What might lie ahead in this area? Here are five ways the latest technology in building customer relationships will change the way we work in the future:[27]

1. Company-wide use of social media: Facebook and similar networks will be used more and more within firms to help remote offices communicate and enable like-minded people in organizations to find each other. It will make people more productive, just as e-mail did back in the nineteen-nineties.
2. E-mail use: E-mail use is declining. Increasingly, there are better tools for collaboration. For example, wikis and instant messages, as well as the social networks mentioned above, are superior to e-mail in a lot of ways. The good thing about some of these functions, too, is that information can be more easily shared and accessed throughout the company than with e-mail.
3. Big Data analysis: Real-time data analysis of social media information will be used more than ever before. The key is not just the collection of these data, but translating them into strategic action. Dashboard programs that put all the data in one place for easy-to-read access will become mainstream.
4. Social media compliance: Morgan Stanley and its 18,000 advisors all joined Twitter. Companies are feeling that they have to get onto social media, but there is also a huge risk of posting something that could lead to a lawsuit. The government and the pharmaceutical

industry remain at very high risk in this area. There are industries opening up for educating people on compliance.

5. Use of international and niche social networks: These are increasing in popularity. "Newer" sites like Instagram and Pinterest are growing exponentially, while the growth rates of the traditional players such as Facebook have almost reached a critical mass. There will be an increasing number of social networks springing up in the future, much as happened with e-mail clients. International outlets pose an interesting challenge for the future. New users in the Asia-Pacific region grew exponentially by 21 percent in 2013. The Chinese version of Twitter, Sina Weibo, had 400 million users in 2014, far more than Twitter's 170 million users.

Chapter Eight

Lesson 7: Be Prepared to Engage in Crisis Management

Marketers have to be prepared for the possibility that things outside their control can have a negative impact on the brand they have worked to build up. Whether they be the result of poorly chosen words, a product-safety concern, or even a natural disaster, these crises cannot be ignored and must be handled carefully. In crises, the position of the brand and the loyalty of consumers are at stake, and the potential damage can be severe. In some cases, however, a well-handled crisis can leave a company or individual in a stronger position than before. This chapter examines crisis management and explores examples of both effective and poor crisis management strategies in some classic cases in both business and politics.

Risk management and risk management strategies are a part of all aspects of business. The number one concern of corporate finance is risk. The designers and operators of a manufacturing facility must consider the safety of their employees as they create a plant. Marketers who create a new toy to be included as a giveaway must consider labeling and the safety of the materials. Human resources departments must perform background and/or drug tests to ensure that the people they employ are unlikely to tarnish the company's image. Cities' requirement to post evacuation plans is a form of risk management. It is extremely difficult to find a single product or service in which risk isn't evaluated in a decision-making process.

It is widely held that risk management can be defined as an economic analysis of three factors: the severity of the threat; the likelihood of occurrence; and the cost to mitigate. When considering severity it is often said that one should "hope for the best and plan for the worst." Even though in many cases the worst-case scenario is an extremely severe and extremely unlikely occurrence which the cost to mitigate is infinite, brand managers should plan ways to mitigate the damage of any threat to the brand that is foreseeable within a possible range of outcomes. For example, take Hurricane Sandy and Hurricane Katrina – two deadly storms that were foreseeable, both of which brought almost total destruction to regions and which were handled with entirely different strategies by two different presidents. In both cases, the severity of the storms was extreme and the likelihood of their impact was near 100 percent and impossible to mitigate. Under circumstances where the crisis is unavoidable and out of the control of anyone, preparedness and response are of the utmost importance in the eyes of consumers, shareholders, and constituents alike.

Crisis Management Issues in Business

The Internet connects people across geographical borders around the world and, through the use of social media, creates the opportunity for dialogue to take place on crises that exist in different countries. Through the sheer power of social media, this new tool forces governments to become more responsive to the crises that crop up around the world, and puts a greater pressure on them to become more transparent and accountable for their actions. In the process, the media effectively become the overseer of all crisis management activities.[1]

Business has become very adept at responding to crises by offering apologies to both its shareholders and society at large. Whenever a crisis occurs, an organization finds itself in the spotlight, under pressure to show itself in the best light possible. If an organization is not able to offer a plausible explanation, owing to adverse circumstances or other issues, such as the inability of an officer to communicate effectively, the next best solution is an apology. So this raises the question of how best to deliver an apology, and how often to repeat it. The fact that apologies are becoming much more commonplace has led some scholars to label this the Age of the Apology. There are of course different ways to offer an apology, from the accused offering an explanation but not requiring the acceptance of the apology by the person(s) affected by the crisis; to offering an apology only after being forced to do so by the offended party; to apologizing in an effort to correct the problem in order to bring closure and mend the relationships that have been strained because of the crisis. The world of politics offers distinctive examples of crises playing out over a long period – with countries at war, for example

– with the added pressure of worldwide attention focused on how political leaders conduct themselves and communicate with one another. The research in this area suggests that the best approach is to try to reach an accord that is accepted by both sides, rather than imposed by one side on the other, with the accompanying risk of perceived humiliation and a backlash that deepens the crisis further.[2]

The field of crisis management has grown out of work carried out in different disciplines, one of which, not surprisingly, is tourism. Influential publications in this field point to the role that the environment plays, in combination with population growth and increased urbanization, in contributing to an increased number of natural disasters and crises. Thierry Pauchant and Ian Mitroff (1992) have defined a crisis as one that physically impacts on a system, thereby threatening the essence of the organization.[3]

The Political Campaign as a Crisis Situation

One of the most interesting "crises" that occurred during the 2012 presidential election centered on Romney's role when he was at Bain Capital, and how the candidate dealt with it.

Throughout the campaign, Romney worked hard at trying to defend the work he carried out at Bain, and attempted to explain to the average voter exactly what a private equity firm does. In his attempt to bolster the notion that the United States has been built on the idea of opportunity for all citizens to live the American Dream, he was hampered by the label of a conservative who was out of touch with the average American. Given the fact that he lost the election, most would have to agree that he was not successful in his explanation of his role, and that it served to create a crisis that he was not able to deal with.[4]

Presidential campaigns begin immediately following the previous campaign. This is certainly true for the election that followed the 2012 campaign, when Governor Chris Christie of New Jersey found himself embroiled in a crisis as he began his preparation for the 2016 presidential cycle. Up until the weekend of 10 January 2014, Christie was considered to be the front runner as the Republican nominee for his party in all opinion polls, and the only Republican candidate who was able to out-poll Hillary Clinton close to three years before the election. That all ended for Christie when he was implicated in a vendetta against a local politician in New Jersey. With the release of information that Governor Christie's long-time and trusted deputy chief of staff, Bridget Anne

Kelly, had written an e-mail that referred to traffic problems in Fort Lee, the crisis began to unfold, resulting in an hour-and-a-half-long press conference by the Governor to try and explain his way of out of the mess and put the blame on his subordinates.

In an effort to deal with the crisis, beyond the news conference, Christie summarily fired Ms. Kelly, whom the Governor had said was as close as family to him. Well, that doesn't sound too good for a presidential candidate who is trying to project an image of a "family man" cut from a different cloth than your typical politician. In fact, that was precisely the strength of the Christie image, the fact that he was seen as a blunt-speaking person who did not conduct vendettas against nonsupporters – in this case, Fort Lee Mayor Mark Sokolich, whom Christie's people were out to hurt because of his lack of support for Christie in the earlier gubernatorial election. The next "head to fall" in this crisis was David Wildstein, a former agency official, who had ordered the lane closures that caused the problem and who took the Fifth Amendment in testimony on 9 January 2014.

Certainly, there are other crises in recent political campaigns that have put a politician in the hot seat, forcing him or her to go on the defensive instead of putting out a positive message to supporters. Other examples are the impeachment of President Bill Clinton and the accusations in 2000 that President George W. Bush had a drinking problem toward the end of his winning campaign against Al Gore. It will become abundantly clear that the crises faced by politicians present an opportunity for marketing managers in the for-profit and nonprofit sectors to gain insight into potential creative solutions to the management and control of crises after they have gone viral.

The Obama Model

Karl Rove and Mitt Romney both lamented that the timing of Hurricane Sandy, taking place right before the election, halted Mitt Romney's progress, while giving Obama an opportunity to shine. Karl Rove wrote a *Wall Street Journal* op-ed piece saying that Obama got "lucky" with Hurricane Sandy, and that Obama won partly because of luck, partly because of running a negative campaign, and partly because of fund raising. On the other hand, some argue that Romney was already losing momentum at the time that Hurricane Sandy hit. Also, 77 percent of Americans praised Obama for acting rapidly in response to the hurricane. Romney, meanwhile, got some negative press as a result of trying to take advantage of the crisis – for example, when he was seen posing for pictures in front of a pile of canned goods.[5]

At the same time, there were foreign policy crises during Obama's first term in office that led some to criticize him for his reactions. For example, the Obama administration's responses to the attacks on the American consulate in Benghazi, Libya, that saw the death of the U.S. ambassador and three other staffers, and to the protests and storming of the U.S. embassy in Cairo, were seen to be weak. In both cases, the attacks were said to be in reaction to a film being produced in the United States that negatively portrayed the Prophet Mohammad. Rather than condemn the attacks, the U.S. embassy released a statement condemning those who try to paint Muslims, or those of any religion, in a negative light. In other words, they condemned the filmmakers, not the attacks. Some have argued that Obama should instead have expressed disapproval of the film and then called for peaceful protests.

One of the biggest crises Obama faced during his first term in office was the economic recession. Many pundits criticized Obama for not reacting strongly enough to the downturn in the economy during his first term in office. In his speeches on the economy, he was known to have used references to the need to "pivot" to jobs, where he maybe should have been more deliberate. Meanwhile, Democrats and Republicans were constantly blaming each other for the problems of the national debt. Some believed that it was the responsibility of the president rather than Congress to offer a plan for the economy and the national debt. The cornerstone of Obama's response was to promise tax increases on the wealthy. However, with all the loopholes in the tax system and the fact that about half of eligible taxpayers don't pay tax, some at the time argued that a strong revamp of the tax system was needed. Even this tactic, however, would not have worked, since Obama increased government spending from 18 percent of GDP to 24 percent during his presidency. Obama did not act on any proposals from the bipartisan Simpson-Bowles commission that was appointed in 2010 to figure out a plan to deal with the fiscal crisis. In fact, some argued that Obama was not doing what he needed to be doing, and he was always either blaming Congress or other people for his inaction.[6]

As one looks back at each of these crises, there is evidence to support the perception that while the President's responses may not have done irreparable damage to his image, he could certainly have done better. By comparison with previous challenges covered in this book, where marketing was used in an innovative manner to overcome obstacles, respond to competition, and help the President succeed in driving public opinion in a desired direction, the challenge of responding to crises requires an even greater understanding of the technology transfer depicted in the Strategic Triad. To fully grasp how Obama was successful in perhaps the greatest crisis of his presidency, Hurricane Sandy, it is important to compare how he handled it with how his predecessor, George W. Bush, handled the greatest crisis of his presidency, Hurricane Katrina. So let's take a closer look at each of those crises and determine why Bush failed and Obama succeeded.

The Case of Katrina

There is little debate that the response to Hurricane Katrina and the perceived lack of preparation was seriously damaging to George W. Bush's image. When the vicious storm struck in 2005, as the nation watched the historic amount of damage it inflicted, President Bush was on vacation at his Texas ranch. Katrina killed 1,833 people and caused over $100 billion in damage. According to the Federal Emergency Management Agency (FEMA), Katrina was the "single most catastrophic natural disaster in U.S. history."[7]

Criticism of the response was widespread. President Bush was assigned the most blame publicly because of his stature and the failures of government officials appointed by him. As it pertains to crisis management, Katrina was both a natural and a political disaster. Since in this case prevention was impossible, we must examine the attempts that were made to mitigate the damage and loss of life and how these efforts were conveyed to the public. In the case of a natural disaster, it is prudent to "hope for the best but plan for the worst" since this type of crisis is completely outside anyone's control. Media coverage of the disaster was primarily focused on the city of New Orleans and the state of Louisiana. As Katrina approached and the storm strengthened over the Gulf of Mexico and as the landfall projections became more accurate, the most obvious solution was to remove people physically from the areas most likely to be affected. During this time, President Bush remained on vacation and mostly out of the public eye. This was a key misstep that negatively influenced how the public perceived the preparedness of the federal government. As head of the Executive Branch, a president is often judged in the same way as a top level corporate executive or CEO. Bush's unwillingness to shorten his vacation in the face of what would prove to be such a destructive force caused him to seem completely out of touch. Generally speaking, the first question asked post-crisis is, "How did we let this happen?" In other words, what was done to prevent this? With Bush on vacation until a full day after the storm had passed, it was easy for those so inclined to equate the lack of preparation with a lack of concern.[8]

From a public relations standpoint, this apparent lack of concern could have played out in one of two ways: Had relief efforts and evacuation plans been well executed, loss of life minimized, and recovery steps executed expeditiously, the lack of concern could have been portrayed as confidence in the preparedness of the government. As we all know, the opposite proved to be true. With each misstep increasing the scrutiny faced by the President, Katrina may have been the biggest public relations debacle in history. According to Kinnon Phillips, the former director of community relations at BP America, the keys to winning the PR battle when facing a disaster are empathy, sincerity,[9] and full disclosure.[10] However, post-Katrina, Bush had already lost his ability to appear empathetic because of the initial perception of his lack of concern. As conditions worsened, the media and other members latched on to the growing sentiment that race and class were issues affecting the timeliness of relief efforts, using this rhetoric to paint Bush as unsympathetic to the conditions faced by the mostly poor and mostly black population affected by the storm.[11] Subsequent federal government efforts to explain why things had gone so poorly were refuted by local government officials in a political game to pin blame. Bush and other government officials made claims regarding preparedness that would later prove to be false, as when on 1 September 2005, Bush said, "I don't think anybody anticipated the breach of the levees," although predictions by the National Weather Service and the National Hurricane Center before the storm made landfall proved to be extremely accurate.[12]

The Case of Sandy

About seven years after Katrina delivered a damaging blow to the legacy of the Bush administration, and as Barack Obama prepared for his bid for re-election in 2012, Hurricane Sandy struck the northeastern United States. Sandy would prove to be the second costliest hurricane in U.S. history, causing widespread damage in the nation's most densely populated area. The storm formed on 22 October 2012 and had dissipated by 31 October, just one week before election day, on 6 November. The storm clearly presented an opportunity for President Obama to prove to the American people that he was a leader who was capable of responding to a crisis of such magnitude.[13]

Politically speaking, Sandy offers an interesting case in crisis management because it occurred during a tightly contested presidential race. The incumbent, Barack Obama, had to be sure that the missteps of Katrina were not repeated; but he also had to appear as though he was not deliberately trying to achieve political gain from a tragedy. The challenger, Mitt Romney, while campaigning for the nation's highest office, knew that a mishandling of the storm by Obama would greatly increase his, Romney's, chance of election, but that to openly criticize the President in the country's time of need would make him appear selfish and that Democrats would have accused him of capitalizing on the suffering of Americans.

Unlike Katrina's effect on President Bush's reputation, Hurricane Sandy created a political windfall of praise and goodwill for President Obama. Republican fundraiser and strategist Karl Rove went so far as to say that the President was "lucky" to have Sandy hit when it did. Rove wrote: "The president was also lucky. This time, the October surprise was not a dirty trick but an act of God. Hurricane Sandy interrupted Mr. Romney's momentum and allowed Mr. Obama to look presidential and bipartisan."[14]

While it might not have been the best choice of words to deem a disaster that devastated so many as a lucky break, the sentiment stands that Obama's effective crisis management may have played a large role in winning over undecided voters in the week leading up to the election. Using the same framework as in the examination of Katrina, we can clearly see that Obama was much more effective than Bush in his execution of the three key elements of crisis management. As with Katrina or any natural disaster, prevention is not an option, and therefore mitigation remains the only possible way to lessen the blow of a hurricane. Obama, though not on vacation, was nevertheless heavily involved in a tightly contested race for the White House. This created a very difficult dilemma: If he spent his time and energy campaigning, Romney could accuse him of abandoning Sandy victims for politics. If he abandoned the campaign, he risked losing a second term in office. However, if he could successfully balance the two challenges, he would be seen to have been effective in leading the country's storm recovery effort, sending a message to voters that his leadership made a difference.

Obama had planned to be visiting neighborhoods that were projected to be hit by the end of the week in the days leading up to the election. The key for Obama was to be seen as making a normal presidential response to a crisis rather than visiting these locations to gain votes. Even John McCain said at the time that he thought the hurricane was a great opportunity for Obama to show presidential leadership during this important week before the election. Romney also responded to the hurricane, but his input was less obvious, as he had no direct control over events. Although he was able to support charities and volunteer centers, he had to be sure not to interfere with relief workers.

Some in the Romney camp did try to turn the storm against Obama in the days leading up to the election, but this proved costly. When Republicans noted that Obama had resumed campaigning, the White House asserted that the President was able to "walk and chew gum at the same time" and was able to point to specific examples in which the President was engaged with the recovery. Not only was there a negative response from media and the public from efforts to politicize the issue, but additionally, it became clear that Obama was seen as doing everything in his power to steer the affected region toward recovery. For Romney, one of the most politically damaging consequences of this tactic was that it drew praise from the Republican governors of the affected states, New Jersey and Virginia, as well as from the mayor of New York City. Governor Chris Christie of New Jersey praised the President for his attentiveness and posted photos of the two talking on the phone to highlight the closeness of their collaboration. Christie said, "The President has been all over this and he deserves great credit." Virginia Governor Bob McDonnell maintained that the federal response was "incredibly fast" and that the President was direct and personal. New York City Mayor Michael Bloomberg endorsed the President, citing the need for a candidate who would address climate change. Obama was elected for a second term, sweeping the Northeast, in part because he had demonstrated to the American public his ability to guide the nation through a trying time.[15]

As these examples show, politics give us an opportunity to see both how damaging a poor crisis management effort can be and the potential rewards of effective leadership. Examination of these two storms provides an "apples-to-apples" comparison, given their occurrence during two different administrations in the same political era. Some crises, however, arise from within. When faced with a crisis resulting from actions within your firm, whether through negligence, malfunction, or just bad luck, the principles remain the same. Show shareholders your company was proactive in trying to prevent the crisis and that you took steps to mitigate the damage when it occurred. Appear prepared and make sure anyone speaking on behalf of the company has the most up-to-date information. Especially ensure that the CEO is able to speak credibly and can outline a clear path to recovery. Be available during recovery and forthright about setbacks. To cover something up will only cause distrust and, worse, give your company a reputation of incompetence. While positioning, branding, and a sense of consumer loyalty are important in establishing a successful organization, crisis management is the skill that will allow a brand to weather a storm and possibly even present an opportunity to enhance its image.

Historic Crises and Corrective Measures

How many people still remember the various food crises or *E. coli* outbreaks over the years? The answer is not many. While the crises do matter, consumers tend not to remember them much, especially if supermarkets convince customers that they've found the source and dealt with it. Even consumer boycotts fade away, as has been seen with Amazon, Google, and Starbucks.

One of the great customer crises took place in the cruise industry when the tour company Carnival's ship was disabled in the Gulf of Mexico following an engine fire. The media tends to shape the message that lingers on with crises of historic proportions. If the media are given everything they need and are treated well, they will stick to a more facts-based approach. However, if the media are treated poorly, as they were with Carnival, they become more critical. Carnival's message was generic and didn't offer any praise for those from the city of Mobile who helped them with their crisis. The overall messaging came off as insincere. Personal pictures from the passengers stranded on the boat also were put on social media, showing a very negative picture of what was going on, and exacerbating Carnival's image problems. Although this was clearly seen as a disaster, Carnival probably will not take a business hit in the long run. Cruises are still very popular, cheap ways for people to take vacations. Nevertheless, other cruise companies should take note and have a crisis plan where empathy and openness are shown and delivered.[16] So, the question is, how could Carnival have responded in a more strategic manner?

The stranded Carnival cruise ship *Triumph* was the third Carnival-owned cruise disaster in a year. The *Costa Concordia* capsized in January 2012 off the coast of Italy. Then a month later, the *Costa Allegra* had an engine fire and lost power in the Indian Ocean where it was vulnerable to pirates. The *Triumph,* as already noted, was stranded in the Gulf of Mexico after the engine caught fire. Sewage was released into the hallways and cabins, food was running out, some passengers were running around "like savages," while most others were scared. Passengers went on social media, posting crazy pictures for the online public to see. To save its image, Carnival should have done the following: First, it should have shown more concern and empathy for the passengers and clearly outlined what it was doing to make things right for them. Second, it should have been more honest, clear, and apologetic in responding to the emergency. Finally, it should have been more prompt in demonstrating and communicating these first two points. Speed matters. This is one area where business can learn from the Obama Model. Obama certainly faced multiple crises during his two campaigns. In fact, a presidential election campaign is constantly in a state of crisis management, and it always pays to get out your message before your opponent does it for you. Obama was consistently aggressive in getting out a message to define his decisions as a president.

In an effort to cut costs, Carnival used only its Twitter account to tweet out updates, rather than taking time and effort and money to get the right people in front of the media and the public. Meanwhile, understandably disgruntled passengers tweeted, and posted tons of pictures and stories of the mayhem as they sat stranded – a glaring example of a company breaking the cardinal rule "Don't let either your competition or your upset customers define the crisis for you."[17]

Another example of a historic crisis was the April 2010 British Petroleum oil spill, following the explosion and sinking of the *Deepwater Horizon* oil rig in the Gulf of Mexico. Whereas BP was seen as having done almost everything wrong in response to the crisis, the company does deserve some credit for doing a few things right. In other words, BP lies somewhere between handling the situation well and handling the situation poorly. The biggest mistake it made was before the crisis even started. It had outsourced a lot of its functions, which it then had no control over. As a result, BP already had a very poor safety record. When Tony Hayward had become CEO in 2007, he had pressed safety issues harder, but ultimately with little success. The whole corporate culture of BP was high risk and high reward, as exemplified by the rush to complete the well even though there were signs prior to the disaster that it was unsafe to do so. The more important lesson, however, is how BP responded after the crisis, and what can be learned from that response.[18]

At first, BP played down the severity of the problem. It probably wasn't as bad as the media portrayed it, but still, BP should have been forthright about the size of the disaster. Although BP ultimately took responsibility for the spill, which, because of contractors, might not have entirely been its fault, if the company had accepted responsibility immediately, it might not have been hurt as badly. Moreover, BP did not push back at its harshest critics – including those in government – as hard as it should have. Even though at times environmental groups stretched the truth in calling out BP, BP didn't condemn the reports or try to prove they were falsehoods. BP continued to claim that safety is its top priority. BP hired the Brunswick Group to be its crisis-consulting firm. The company also retained lobbyists with connections to Democrats and Republicans, and continued to donate to their campaigns, which was probably not a bad idea.[19]

Never Lie about a Crisis

If an organization is dealing with a crisis that threatens its reputation, it should never lie. This is what the Susan J. Komen Foundation did as it tried to deal with the Planned Parenthood debacle. Lying does several things that eventually work against an organization in crisis: It offends your supporters' intelligence; undermines your supporters' relationships with you; shows that you are stupid; makes people wonder what else you're lying about; makes people see you as an organization in denial; distracts you from actually controlling the damage and fixing the situation; embarrasses your employees; prevents your organization from learning; and makes you unforgivable.[20]

The Susan G. Komen for the Cure foundation found itself in difficulties over the highly polarizing issue of abortion. The decision to pull back funding from Planned Parenthood through a change in the definition of the foundation's grant guidelines, only to reverse the decision after public outcry (especially on social media), left Komen in a really bad position with both ideological wings of its supporters. Komen released an apology saying that its main mission is to save women's lives, and its decision to pull back funding went against that. Planned Parenthood provides reproductive health care, sex education, breast cancer screenings, and other services, not only abortions, which is why so much attention was generated against Komen's withdrawal of funding from Planned Parenthood. Komen eventually amended its funding criteria to allow the inclusion of Planned Parenthood. Planned Parenthood President Cecile Richards responded that Planned Parenthood was very happy that Komen had reversed its decision. Richards also announced that she was confident that Komen was fully behind her organization. Planned Parenthood gets about $700,000 a year from Komen to help fund mammograms and breast exams. The Komen decision to pull funding led to about $3 million in new donations for Planned Parenthood. Donors included Michael Bloomberg, who gave $250,000, and Lance Armstrong, who donated $100,000 through his LiveStrong foundation. Komen remained steadfast with its statement that politics hadn't played a role in the changes to its funding guidelines and called the crisis a misunderstanding of its funding policies, but the PR fiasco clearly hurt the organization.[21]

Pennsylvania State University is another example of an organization that lied about a scandal it was embroiled in. The university botched the handling of sexual assault allegations against coach Jerry Sandusky. The school's president, Graham Spanier, declared his support for administrator Gerry Schultz and athletic director Tim Curley, who were charged with neglecting to report the sexual assault charges against Sandusky. Penn State's long-serving football coach Joe Paterno said he was shocked at the allegations. The university should have made statements that could have somewhat exonerated the school, or at least prevented it from getting into worse trouble. Perhaps the most shocking thing was the comments by Spanier and Paterno, which prompted the questions how Spanier could have supported the two officials who had neglected to do the jobs they were hired to do and how Paterno could have claimed to be "shocked" by a situation that had been under investigation for two years. Penn State appeared to be trying to brush the controversy aside by saying that questions during Paterno's press conference would be limited to football questions. Penn State could have dealt with the scandal in the right way. Instead, the university's actions made things worse, leaving a brand that had once had a terrific image tarnished for many years to come.[22]

Issues to Consider When Implementing a Crisis Solution

A company's leaders should be ready to stand before shareholders or the public and acknowledge the crisis, lay out a plan for recovery, and help calm the nerves of the parties who are affected. Executives who go into hiding simply encourage negative speculation to run rampant.

Executives must be well briefed and knowledgeable about all aspects of the company affected by and responsible for a crisis. They also need to provide up-to-date, accurate information about the situation. By sharing the latest developments, they project authority and become the "go-to" person for more information. This represents a proactive approach to crisis management – the approach taken by Obama in dealing with the aftermath of Hurricane Sandy. Even if there's been a negative development, if the source of the bad news is the chief executive, the message is sent that the company is aware of it and already taking steps to get the situation under control. There are times when a leadership change is the only way to dispel criticism and mistrust, and this was well spelled out in the discussion of BP. This is the one area where there is a difference between the political sector and other sectors, as removing Obama from his position as candidate in 2008, or president in 2012, was never an option.[23]

As with all cases requiring risk management, the first step is to assess the size of the risk, including in worst-case scenarios, to determine how likely each scenario is to play out and estimate both the cost of mitigating the risk and the cost of failing to do so. Once that has been done, the CEO, as company spokesperson, should be very forthright about both good developments and bad, and should also present an action plan immediately. Quick action reduces the incentive for media and shareholders to probe for more details and allows the firm to spend its time and energy in managing the crisis rather than managing the media. Finally, failing to admit accountability and trying to shift responsibility will only provoke a response from the blamed party. Attempting to put the blame on someone else often invites closer scrutiny and makes it more difficult to address the problem. A better approach is to identify the source of the problem and reassure the public that steps are being taken to control it and prevent it from happening again.[24]

It is critical that a positive course of action that addresses all facets of the crisis as fully as possible be presented at an early stage. Avoid the image of an executive who is debating what to do, even if it means disclosing that all relevant information is still not available. In the midst of a crisis, firms need to be seen as decisive. As information becomes available, it must continue to be the CEO who presents it at press conferences, to reinforce the image of someone with confidence and in control. Finally, it is a good practice to bring industry consultants or politicians into the loop and have them publicly endorse your plan of action. Having other trusted voices endorse a plan or collaborate with the chosen approach sends the message that the company is doing everything it can. Recall that President Obama brought in Governor Chris Christie during the Hurricane Sandy crisis to signal support for his actions.[25]

Ultimately, a crisis presents an opportunity for dynamic change leadership. During a crisis, stakeholders will be engaged and willing to consider initiatives that they may not have otherwise considered. During noncrisis times, it will be more difficult to bring about dramatic change, as it may be perceived as fixing something that isn't broken or rocking the boat. Crises present a unique opportunity for a chief executive to prove his or her ability to be dynamic and able to adapt to new circumstances. As the crisis moves forward, it may call for the appointment of a spokesperson who is well trained and well informed to control the information that is disseminated. Effective leadership will also call for the inclusion of trusted representatives of those who are affected to project empathy and understanding of the seriousness of the crisis. It is imperative that the action plan decided upon at the beginning of the crisis continue to unfold in a clear and unambiguous manner, which means the avoidance of confusing public statements at all costs.

Crises Are Inevitable in All Sectors

There are many ways to deal with a crisis, although most responders do it poorly. Kevin Burke, the chairman, president, and CEO of Consolidated Edison, New York's power supplier, botched the PR job with the summer's heat wave (in 2006). During a ten-day summer outage, he didn't show up until near the end of the crisis, when he told people that he didn't know how it had happened. This didn't help him win any fans, nor did it add to his credibility. New York Mayor Rudy Giuliani's handling of the 9/11 attacks was the correct way to handle a crisis. So was Michael Bloomberg's handling of the subway strike during the winter of 2005, which had him walking to work along with other New York City residents. Leaders need to show up, make apologies, empathize, and give honest explanations. In 2006, then CEO of BP Bob Malone apologized to Alaskans for having to shut down a damaged oil pipeline, and was praised for it. However, it then became apparent that BP had received lots of warnings about the damaged pipeline but had done nothing about them. So Mr. Malone looked as if he was trying to deceive the public, and was worse off than before. To deal with crises, companies need to pre-plan by setting up an investigation team that will look at the causes of the crisis and how similar crises can be prevented in the future. A communications team needs to be set up as well. Then scenarios need to be practiced to see how the team deals with crisis.[26]

Many companies prepare for crises, and even run through scenarios. However, when a real crisis hits, they are still often unprepared. According to Caroline Sapriel, head of crisis management consultancy CS&A, disasters call for a command-and-control type of leadership style, which doesn't happen often with organizations today, which tend to be oriented toward consensus. Basically, companies have to be honest with themselves and prepare for the worst. It is interesting to compare the corporate world, where crisis usually spells the end for the management team, no matter how they handle the crisis, with the political world, where if a politician navigates a crisis, it can elevate him or her to stardom. With BP in 2010, the CEO Tony Hayward was the media focal point and took the brunt of the blame for the disaster. He ended up resigning after a few PR blunders, including under-reporting the severity of the disaster and being photographed on his yacht during the middle of the crisis. Basically, a CEO who is in the spotlight too much will eventually make mistakes. The key is getting a good balance between being too visible and not visible enough. Clichés are a hazard. The media may be portrayed as taking things too far and looking for conspiracy theories. The company, on the other hand, is likely to be accused of trying to downplay the situation. The company itself may have limited information about what is going on, so the best approach is to be as open as possible and keep the information flowing. If a company denies the obvious, or lies, it will suffer. The true purpose of any crisis management, however, is dealing with the problem, and fixing it – not trying to control the media.[27]

In all crises involving corporations, leaders need to know what's going on and who's accountable, portray a confident, "it's-under-control" type of coolness, and be realistic and have a plan for the future. BP CEO Tony Hayward did not do any of these things. He didn't show empathy to those affected by the oil spill; he told a Congressional panel that he was "out of the loop" about the decisions on the rig, and he kept understating the magnitude of the spill. Other companies can learn from this. First of all, the CEO is the public face of the company. The CEO should at least be trained on how to appear empathetic and project an air of assurance that the company is on top of everything. The company needs to know how to manage its image or brand, and having a CEO who is well prepared to handle disasters or crises is part of this brand management. Second, it is imperative to know what's going on in the company. The CEO can't know every corner of the company intimately, especially with large corporations like BP. That's why it's important during crises to have the CEO be familiar at least with what's going on in the front lines. CEOs can then at least talk about how things really are, and appear that they are in control. Finally, it's important to know when the CEO needs to step down. During the BP oil spill, knowing when to have the CEO step down was of symbolic as well as practical importance, also indicating that the company was serious about taking responsibility for the crisis.[28]

Crisis management experts agree that in times of crisis it's imperative to focus less on working with your head and more on working with your heart. Business schools use BP as an example of how not to conduct crisis management. From the beginning, Tony Hayward blundered, including by downplaying the seriousness of the disaster, denying to Congress that he had any part in the planning of the well, and commenting that he "wanted his life back," which was perceived as callous, detached, and selfish, and concerned only with how the crisis affected his own comfort. Instead, he should have apologized to and empathized with those who had suffered from the disaster, including the eleven rig workers who died and their families. BP also did not lay out a plan that showed how it was going to deal with the spill. The company seemed to blame the government and to be withholding information about how bad the problem was. BP needed to manage the situation by communicating better with the public, including constant and full disclosure. It should have tried to build up a rapport with the media and the community, and when it didn't, rumors swirled that it had no chance to squelch, whether they were true or false. Communicating and building relationships could have mitigated some of this, as well as buying the company more time to deal with the situation. (Exxon, to this day, is still trying to live down the memory of the *Exxon Valdez* oil spill of 1989. People still remember that issue.)[29]

There are several ways to handle a crisis and take care of your company's image. As summarized by Davia Temin in *Forbes* magazine, these include the following: Assume all of the facts will be uncovered, and don't try to hide anything; keep your emotions in check; keep focused on how other people see you and your company; move quickly, and do the right things; learn what the right tone of your message should be; don't lie by publicly denying something, unless it really is untrue; try to achieve a balance between showing humility and humanity versus keeping your liability limited; use the crisis to get your morals straight; apologize, and figure out how you'll avoid that mistake in future; be part of the solution, not the problem; start getting recognized for positive things so your crisis will be forgotten; and finally, don't repeat your mistake.[30]

Chapter Nine

Concluding Remarks

The marketing lessons reported in this book rest on the contribution of the Obama Model as it was implemented in the two presidential campaigns the Obama team successfully ran in 2008 and 2012. Each of the election campaigns relied on a knowledge of basic marketing techniques and strategies that can be found in use in any organization that seeks to understand and respond to its customers and deliver a value proposition in the form of a product or a service. But this is where the similarity ends! As marketing case studies, the Obama campaigns demonstrate the integrative use of technological advances for the first time in a marketplace setting, establishing a new set of best practices for organizations in both the corporate and nonprofit worlds. The marketing lessons that have been laid out in chapters 2 through 8 of this book rely to a greater or lesser degree on the use of technological advances that, in some cases, have been available since the 1980s but, until their use by the Obama teams in both campaigns, had not been leveraged for maximum effect. Both John McCain in 2008 and Mitt Romney in 2012 lost in large part because their campaign organizations did not understand and apply the latest technological developments from several related fields to their respective marketing strategies.

The Obama Model is best understood by taking into account the technology transfer that was outlined in the Strategic Triad presented in chapter 2. The Strategic Triad integrates three innovative technology advances that are used by political, corporate, and nonprofit organizations in often distinct ways. These innovations are micro-targeting, social media, and Big Data. Each lesson discussed is based on examples from organizations that have developed a marketing strategy that makes use of these three innovations to a greater or lesser degree. The degree of sophistication of the use of these innovative practices in each sector is the result of the stage of the evolution of the marketing life cycle in each of those industries, as well as the resources available and the need to follow the marketing concept in each one.

The main argument put forward in this book is that the application of marketing to politics has evolved over approximately sixty years. In each decade from the 1950s to the present, presidential campaigns have relied on a technology transfer that reflected the "state of the art" at the time the campaign was run. The two most recent campaigns, in 2008 and 2012, represent a paradigm shift in the use of marketing in politics that can now be applied to the profit and nonprofit sectors in both mature industries and start-ups. The Obama Model in effect represents the lessons from one of the most successful start-ups in the history of marketing.

For example, in the political marketplace, where campaign organizations are dealing with citizens who may or may not choose to vote, the imperative is to get customers, in this case voters, to exercise their legal right to cast a ballot for a candidate. The marketing imperative in this sector is to get a citizen interested in the campaign of a candidate running for office and then convert that interest into the act of voting for that particular politician. In an effort to implement a marketing strategy in politics, the same goal holds here as it does in any other marketplace, and that is the ability to define value for the voter, and then present a product, or in this case a service offered by the politician, that is attractive enough to win over the voter and keep that person loyal, both up to the election and afterward when the leader is in office.

The same principle holds true on the commercial side, but with a slight twist. The marketing challenge is to offer value, win over the customer, beat out your competition, and then hold onto that customer for life, if possible. However, in the case of a customer buying a product or using a service of some kind, a corporation may find itself in the unique position of having that customer seek out the corporation instead of the corporation seeking out the customer. In the case of a political campaign, citizens do not have to vote to survive, pay their bills, or enjoy their chosen lifestyle, so the marketing effort is slightly different. This is not to say that corporations do not seek to build on their customer base and increase their loyal following; however, corporate marketing is based on a different value proposition, and may necessitate the use of different media and distribution channels to connect with the customer.

The nonprofit sector is different again; the marketing challenge there is to get people to volunteer their time and money and the other resources necessary to keep alive an organization that seeks to help people in need or distress. Reaching out to people who are sensitive to the plights of others calls for establishing emotional connections with the target customer base. This requirement is not as critically important to the success of a for-profit organization as it is to that of a nonprofit. Again, the imperative is the same, but the delivery of value may be very different because of the nature of the value proposition.

This brings us to the structure of the Strategic Triad, which is set up to show that each of the technological tools may be used in unique ways in different markets by different organizations, as each finds its own creative solutions to its individual challenges. As illustrated in this book, advances in technology and marketing transferred from the corporate world to the political world between 1952 and the first Obama campaign have produced significant changes in politics.[1]

From the campaign of Dwight Eisenhower in 1952 through to the campaign of George W. Bush in 2004, we have witnessed successive uses of the latest marketing advances that have proven to be decisive in presidential victories. Whether by relying on the latest advances in advertising, polling, marketing research, branding, positioning, or database technologies, each successive campaign borrowed the latest technological tools from the corporate world and used them to stay competitive in the political marketplace. It was the pressure to respond to an increasingly competitive global marketplace that motivated corporations to determine how best to respond to customer needs and wants. The pressure of competition also influenced political campaigns, as Democrats and Republicans alike came to the realization that party identification could no longer be taken for granted, and that voters were beginning to rely on different sources of information through new channels to choose their leader, and in some cases were defecting from their earlier party allegiance. At the same time, demographic shifts in the U.S. population made it more difficult for political organizations to succeed with the tactics and strategies that had proved successful before 1952. This is why and how the field of political marketing became established as a field of inquiry, seeking to document the marketing challenges facing political organizations and devise new strategies to help candidates win office and enable leaders to influence public opinion.[2]

The Obama campaigns demonstrated the importance of putting experts in all related fields in marketing around the same table – experts who understood how to integrate the use of micro-targeting, social media, and Big Data and analytics to define and deliver value for citizens and voters. The chapters in this book highlight the direction of the technology transfer from each of the three sectors and use examples of successful companies from a broad cross-section of organizations in all three sectors to reinforce the lesson of each chapter. The examples also show, however, that there is still room in all organizations, in both the corporate and nonprofit sectors, to achieve further gains by following more closely the use of innovative marketing in the Obama teams' campaigns.

Micro-targeting

All marketing campaigns, whether they are directed at voters, consumers, or volunteers, need to use micro-targeting in order to follow the marketing concept. Micro-targeting continues to grow as a methodology for several reasons. First of all, while in politics it is used to increase voter turnout and identify better information about the values of voters, in other sectors it can be helpful to any organization seeking to increase its market share. Second, as the cost to run television advertising continues to stay high, especially for start-up companies or those that need to watch their budget carefully, it can help them avoid waste and target messages to only those people likely to have an interest in the organization's product or service. Third, it helps companies get a better measure of exactly who their customers are and why they choose to do business with their organization and gives them a base market for future offerings. Fourth, as more and more people are moving their media viewing from television to online videos such as YouTube and other social media sites, micro-targeting will be a key tool in reaching these audiences more effectively.

In the Obama campaign organization, the use of micro-targeting was carried out by many different members of the team, including consultants, public relations advisors, and media advisors. The conclusion of many experts is that the 2012 campaign was the year that online political advertising matured – as television advertising matured in the 1960s, when the famous Daisy commercial run by the Johnson campaign introduced the power of advertising to the electorate. Although advertising on the Internet has been omnipresent since the 1990s, the Howard Dean campaign in 2004 and the Obama campaign in 2008 made quantum leaps in this area.

There were some material differences in the application of micro-targeting techniques between the two Obama campaigns. Although micro-targeting was a relatively new concept in 2004, in 2008 it became an integral part of every aspect of the Obama campaign, from the caucuses to the general election. In 2012 there was an even bigger difference with respect to working with online data. On the Republican side, Romney used much more sophisticated micro-targeting tactics than McCain had in 2008. (The big challenge now in reaching voters is citizens' use of call-forwarding, caller ID, and privacy managers to avoid being reached by telephone.) The advances made in the 2012 campaign enabled the campaign to use online space in real time, meaning it might take only a few days as opposed to a few weeks to get information back from a survey and analyze the data to build a database of prospective voters. Quantitative analysis of the micro-targeted data provided the team with a powerful tool, allowing them to attach "scores" to voters that identified them as either more or less likely to be open to influence.

In 2012, Obama, on a consistent basis, won the right districts in states he needed to win in the election, in some cases resulting in very narrow victories in terms of the popular vote. This reflected the overall strategy of the Obama team, which was to win the right votes in the right places. It should not be surprising to know that other candidates running in the 2012 election did their own calculations on exactly which districts they needed to win to get enough electoral votes for victory. The big difference is that the Obama team started using analytics very early on and continued to use it throughout the campaign. The Obama team consistently responded to any changes in all forms of data collected by polling, on the website, and on social networks, and had the flexibility to move resources into districts where its messages were resonating with voters. A testament to this strategy lies in the numbers: Obama won the election based on electoral votes with approximately a 30 percent margin, but with just a 3 percent margin in the popular vote.

Social Media

Social media strategies are most effective when they create an interaction with individual consumers. The Obama team understood this and put initiatives into play that engaged the public. The Obama White House held "town hall" meetings via Twitter to address a wide range of subjects. Through reddit.com, the President addressed questions in what is known as an AMA (Ask Me Anything) format spanning a very broad cross-section of subjects. The AMA sessions were so popular that they jammed the Internet because Reddit servers had never before been exposed to so much traffic. At the suggestion of one of his top aides, Obama even used "in" lingo from Reddit when he ended a response with "NOT BAD" (a common response used by Redditors); the capital letters were his choice. In his sign-off message he mentioned the importance of registering to vote and plugged gottaregister.com. Within the next day 30,000 people had visited gottaregister.com despite the President's failure to hyperlink the text. Upon reviewing the data, the team also found that more than 5.2 million people had visited the thread, making it the most trafficked thread in Reddit's history.

This example also highlights the importance of agility, which is becoming an increasingly vital attribute of a successful marketing strategy centered on social media. For the first time in history, firms are now able to "listen" in on the public in real time as they react to events. Companies are now able to listen to the interaction taking place between their customers and the various social media sites and pick up on the chatter and tone of the conversation. As mentioned earlier, when Clint Eastwood addressed an empty seat that was meant to represent the President at the 2012 Republican National Convention, within minutes of Eastwood's leaving the stage, "Invisible Obama" was a Twitter account with 6,000 followers, and the hash-tag #Eastwooding flooded the Twitter feed. By 9:30 p.m., Obama himself had tweeted a response – a photo of him in a White House chair captioned, "This seat's taken."

Social media campaigns can also be used very effectively to raise funds, something that nonprofit organizations must do on a regular basis. Fund raising was one of the key uses of social media in the 2012 election campaign, with the Obama team using some surprising tactics based on analysis of its data about potential contributors. The "Dinner with Barack" contests that featured George Clooney and the President at one event and *Sex and the City* star Sara Jessica Parker and the President at another were notable examples. The use of celebrities is nothing new to the corporate world, but the huge success of it on the political side suggests that there may be opportunities that can still be tapped by organizations seeking to raise funds.

The Obama teams also used social media to encourage voters to become advocates for Obama (i.e., to get others out to vote), an important element in the success of his campaigns. His message was centered on the community, people, and change, not Barack Obama. This is an important lesson to all organizations that use social media – they need to focus on sending out a message that is all about the people reading it, and not the organization sending it out. The messages sent out by Obama were vague yet universally meaningful, allowing people to construct meaning in their own ways. The Obama campaign also built trust by being transparent, and by using all possible social media platforms. The campaign urged followers to post, share, and get involved in any way they could. This enabled followers to effectively create their own campaign.

Whereas social networks are set up to have a two-way conversation with voters, both Obama and Romney tended to use communication only in a one-way broadcast style. The only area where Obama let citizen voices be heard was on his blog, where the content could be controlled. Perhaps this is the key difference between the political and nonpolitical marketplaces: the potential, in politics, for a response to do unanticipated damage to the organization sending it out. Another area where the political and nonpolitical sectors differ is that messages in the political sector may focus more on the competition. About 33 percent of Romney's content was about Obama, whereas Obama only talked about Romney 14 percent of the time. In July before the election, however, Obama's content did start focusing more on Romney than it had before. Unfortunately, in the United States, negative advertising still plays a major role in the communications between a campaign organization and voters.

Big Data and Analytics

Big Data effectively becomes the glue that allows an organization to carry out micro-targeting campaigns. Although large databases have existed for close to thirty years, it is only recently that experts and computer analytics could be brought together to harness this technology. Thirty years ago, in the mid-1980s, although this new technology showed much promise, the analytics were not there to support it. It was clear at the outset that measuring and tracking sales records and other relevant metrics could provide information a company could use to build relationships with its customers and suppliers. Today, in large part because of the innovative use of this technology in the Obama 2008 and 2012 campaigns, any organization can gain access to information about all aspects of our lives with the click of a computer mouse.

Obama's campaign director in 2008, David Plouffe, said that the goal of the campaign was not only to ensure high participation and turnout of the Democrats' base but also to expand the size of the electorate by mobilizing first-time voters, mainly among young adults and minorities. In its effort to accomplish the goal set by Plouffe, the team focused on the Internet and text message strategies, sending out more than 1 billion e-mails over the course of the campaign, and effectively turning my.barackobama.com (the URL during the campaign) into a key strategic weapon. This methodology was taken to a new level by the Obama team in 2012, in part by implementing a "rule" that all decisions were to be based on measurable data. Although the 2008 campaign was data driven, the strategy in 2012 extended this thinking even further. For example, the campaign gathered as many as 1,000 variables of information on each voter, obtained from voter registration records, consumer data warehouses, and prior campaign contacts. To obtain this information, the Obama team turned to both public and private databases, some of which had been available for as much as two decades but were now being mined to new purpose in 2012. Sophisticated use of this information contributed to the success of the team's microtargeting efforts in predicting which advertising campaigns would be the most successful.

Along with these mega-databases, persuasion scores were developed to enable the campaign to focus its communication efforts and use volunteers manning the telephone banks to contact voters who were likely to transfer their vote to the Democrats. The scores also were used to determine which appeals to put into the ad campaigns. The campaign realized that one telephone call alone might not change a voter's mind, but that several calls might do so. As part of the experimentation that was used to measure the effectiveness of all strategic aspects of the campaign, tests were done to determine how long the persuasion effect lasted after the first phone call (and it was found to be about three weeks). The key lesson for political marketers is that the correct database with the right algorithms can be used to powerful effect to fill in data gaps with intelligent assumptions based on the right mix of information. This insight was perhaps the most important contribution of the Obama campaigns to marketing know-how that will benefit organizations in all business sectors, both for-profit and nonprofit, for many years to come.

Beyond Obama

To date, there has not been a comprehensive analysis of the role of marketing in the two Obama campaigns. There has been a lot written on the role of social media and the Internet, but these are only two examples of how technology has moved into every aspect of marketing, driving all organizations to take the approach of the Obama teams, an approach based on breaking down departmental barriers and encouraging the experts responsible for a company's marketing success to sit at the same table and talk and work with one another. The Obama Model proves that this is possible. In learning from it, the typical corporation can find ways to weather crises (as discussed in chapter 8), by putting in place appropriate marketing models before any crisis hits. A presidential campaign, by definition, is constantly in a crisis mode and must be on the alert 24/7 to any challenges from an opponent. For that matter, running a government in what we have referred to as the "permanent campaign" makes all of the marketing tools discussed in this book relevant to a president who must constantly be ready for the next crisis to hit.[3]

This leads us to consider what will happen after Obama leaves office and how political parties and organizations in the for-profit and non-profit sectors might use the cutting-edge thinking put forward in this book. It is clear that there will be continued demand for and use of Big Data as candidates amass and mine an ever-growing wealth of information. This is the future of all marketing campaigns – the constant building up of the most detailed information in order to influence the attitudes, intentions, and behavior of individual voters and customers. Ultimately, the role of any marketing campaign is to link a person's hopes and dreams to a particular product or service, be it a political candidate or a pair of Nike shoes, portraying a better tomorrow for the consumer of the product or the supporter of the candidate.

The American Dream in 2014

So where was "the American Dream" for citizens of the United States in 2014? This topic was addressed in a *Wall Street Journal* opinion piece by Mortimer Zuckerman, editor-in- chief of *U.S. News & World Report*.[4] Zuckerman's view was that the American Dream was quickly evaporating, with many Americans feeling that conditions in the United States were not fair to the average American. He went on to point out some statistics, such as that the share of financial compensation going to labor had dropped to 60 percent in 2014 from 65 percent before 1980. He also noted that in 2014, 48 million people in the United State worked in low-wage jobs, and that, according to the Bureau of Labor Statistics, there were approximately 91 million people over the age of sixteen who weren't working, a new high for that statistic. He argued that the United

States in 2014 was going through the weakest post-recession recovery in the history of the country. This brings us to the post-Obama period, where the leaders who take over the country in 2016 and beyond will have to rely on the tenets put forward in this book, which emphasize the importance of building an emotional connection between government and citizens, founded on hoping and trusting that their leaders can fix a broken economy and build a strong future for their children and grandchildren.

The Technology Can Still Be Improved

Despite their increasing reliance on the advanced technologies described in this book, the pollsters got it wrong in the 2014 mid-term elections. The Republican victories all across the country were a surprise to many citizens; but perhaps no one was more surprised than the pollsters themselves. Throughout the country, pre-election polls suggested that Democratic candidates were neck-and-neck with their Republican rivals. This was even true for the "polls of polls," such as the Real Clear Politics aggregate of all polls, which also got it wrong. In part, the pollsters' failure was the result of inaccurate measures of how many citizens would actually go out and vote. As it turned out, turnout was very low all over the country, a factor that was missed by most pollsters. The argument put forward by some pollsters in defense of their lapse was that voters are embarrassed to report their intention not to vote, and often lie about it when questioned in a poll.[5]

This is a fundamental challenge for marketers in any marketplace, whether political, for-profit, or nonprofit – there is a difference between what people think they will do and what they say they will do. The reliability of marketers' information is dependent on the truthfulness of the respondents surveyed. That said, it is important to understand the real contribution of marketing to politics – or any other enterprise, for that matter. Marketing must be seen as a discipline that, at its best, is able to provide an insight into the future decision making of a voter or consumer. Without knowledge of what an organization can expect from its promotional efforts in a market, it will not pay for any company to spend advertising or promotional dollars to reinforce or change people's thinking or behavior. Which brings us back to the pollsters' mispredictions in the 2014 mid-term elections. Sophisticated technologies notwithstanding, we must always allow for the fact that the psychology of human behavior is very complicated, and without an accurate assessment of the context, no model can be expected to work perfectly.

The Future

In the future I believe the Obama campaigns will be seen as a turning point in the application of marketing tools, with lessons applicable to the twenty-first-century challenges facing all organizations. Of course, there are risks associated with any new technology – risks of misuse or overuse and of media misunderstanding of the role these methods play in the interaction between citizens and governments or consumers and corporations.[6]

A question that arises is what will the next "movement" be in the United States?

As movements continue to emerge all over the world, they will rely more and more on the integration of technological methods with marketing knowledge to bring people together in a cohesive and unified manner and give them a voice. How will mobile technologies and other advances in this area affect future campaigns, whether political, or commercial, or humanitarian? The odds are that they will play a very significant role in becoming the newest "channel" of communication that allows leaders and organizations in all sectors to keep connected to their constituencies, of whatever type. We are moving toward a world where it will be impossible for organizations to be effective without an understanding of the latest marketing technology in their industry, or without a "cross-sectoral" approach to marketing that enables them to adapt ideas from one sector for use in another.

There are lessons to be learned from politicians' use of the technologies employed by corporations and nonprofits on a regular basis. This is an underdeveloped area in marketing that needs to be studied, by scholars and practitioners alike, to help us perfect the tools we use to achieve our political, commercial, or humanitarian goals. For too long, books about marketing have focused primarily on strategies for promoting consumer products and services. The marketing strategy in the 2008 and 2012 presidential campaigns, referred to as the Obama Model, provides a new and different perspective on the use of the latest and most sophisticated marketing methods and technologies. It may well inspire the development of innovative MBA programs that educate our students and future business leaders in the "cutting-edge" marketing practices they will need to compete in an increasingly complex, interconnected world.

A Vision for America: The Restoration of the American Dream (Delivered to Senior Aides to President Clinton in the White House on 20 March 1995)

The Challenge facing the president is to move public opinion in the direction that he thinks is best for the country. The president has not been successful in his attempts to achieve this challenge for two reasons: (a) the lack of a cohesive message that connects to the concerns of most Americans, that is, future economic security for them and their children and no hope of achieving their America Dream, and (b) the use of improper channels of communication to convey his accomplishments to the American people. Citizens are looking to the president to present them with a vision for America, one that connects with their hearts and minds. The restoration of the American Dream is a vision that can make the president successful in this regard.

- It is a vision that applies to everyone.
- It has both an emotional and a rational appeal.
- It will serve as an "informational anchor" to which Americans can connect the legislation the president initiates.
- It can be used to break down the American electorate on the basis of benefits that government offers to all people.

The vision is best communicated by using three channels of communication, with appeals determined by a nationwide segmentation analysis of the electorate. The results of the analysis will identify what the American Dream means to various political and sociodemographic groups in society.

1. A prime-time news conference should be held to announce the president's new vision to the American people. This venue should

be repeated as often as possible to update the American people on the successful implementation of the vision.

2. Regional "American Dream Summits" should be held around the country to generate an excitement and interest in the president's new vision by interest groups and the media, the two key groups of leaders who will help communicate the message to the public.

3. Empower "well-respected" opinion leaders (e.g., community and religious leaders, educators, local government officials) who will rely on word of mouth to build up a grassroots channel in addition to using talk radio and other more traditional media.

This strategy will work because it allows the president to talk about himself in a personal and positive way to which average Americans can relate. The president can define himself as someone who has lived the American Dream, working his way up from the bottom to the top, and who is now the leader of the free world (instead of letting the competition define him as a Democrat).

Notes

Introduction

1 See Wojciech Cwalina, Andrzej Falkowski, & Bruce I. Newman, *Political Marketing: Theoretical and Strategic Foundations* (London: M.E. Sharpe, 2011) for a model that explains how the permanent campaign is used in politics.

2 Wojciech Cwalina, Andrzej Falkowski, & Bruce I. Newman, "Political Management and Political Marketing," in D.W. Johnson (Ed.), *Handbook of Political Management*, 67–80 (London: Routledge, 2009).

3 Philip J. Davies & Bruce I. Newman (Eds.), *Winning Elections with Political Marketing* (London: Routledge, 2006).

4 Richard Robbins, "Marketing Lessons from Election '12',"*Huffington Post*, 13 November 2012.

5 In a meeting with Erskine Bowles, then deputy chief of staff to President Clinton, in the White House, I was informed of the magnitude of the job of the president as we discussed strategies to get the president re-elected.

6 See Bruce I. Newman, *The Marketing of the President: Political Marketing as Campaign Strategy* (Thousand Oaks, CA: Sage Publications, 1994) for a historical overview of this discipline.

7 Bruce I. Newman, *The Mass Marketing of Politics: Democracy in an Age of Manufactured Images* (Thousand Oaks, CA: Sage Publications, 1999).

8 Newman, *The Marketing of the President.*

9 Bruce I. Newman, *Handbook of Political Marketing* (Thousand Oaks, CA: Sage Publications, 1999), xiii. For a review of the discipline of political marketing, see: Wayne Steger, Sean Kelly, & Mark Wrighton (Eds.), *Campaigns and Political Marketing* (New York: Routledge, 2006); Paul Baines (Ed.), *Political Marketing* (London: Sage Publications, 2011); Cwalina, Falkowski, & Newman, *Political Marketing: Theoretical and Strategic Foundations.*

10 Ibid.
11 Philip Kotler, *Marketing Management* (New York: Prentice-Hall, 2011).
12 Wojciech Cwalina, Andrzej Falkowski, & Bruce I. Newman, *A Cross-Cultural Theory of Voter Behavior* (New York and London: The Haworth Press, Taylor & Francis Group, 2008), 70.
13 H.F. Goldglantz, "Marketing Matters When Strategies Match Tactics," *Management Professional*, 81(10) (2013): 68.
14 B.H. Meredith, "Where Politics and Marketing Meet (but Shouldn't)," *NZ Business*, 27(11) (2013): 52.
15 R. Wollan, "How to Keep Customers? Mix Old Strategies with New Tactics," *Advertising Age* (February 2013). Retrieved from http://adage.com/article/cmo-strategy/customers-mix-strategies-tactics/240001/.
16 A. Pierce, "Yes, Your Brand Can Become a Challenger – It's Not That Hard," *Advertising Age* (December 2013). Retrieved from http://adage.com/article/cmo-strategy/channel-challenger-mindset/245780/.

1 The Evolution of Marketing in Politics

1 Bruce I. Newman, *The Marketing of the President: Political Marketing as Campaign Strategy* (Thousand Oaks, CA: Sage Publications, 1994).
2 Lou Harris, *Is There a Republican Majority?* (New York: Harper & Brothers, 1954).
3 This is well documented by Newman in *The Marketing of the President*.
4 Karl Rove, "National Tea Party Groups Take a Beating," *Wall Street Journal*, 26 June 2014: A13.
5 For a thorough review of the use of social media in the 2008 Obama campaign, see: Costas Panagopoulos (Ed.), *Strategy, Money and Technology in the 2008 Presidential Election* (New York: Routledge, 2011).
6 "Marketing Lessons from Team Obama". Available at: http://www.mediapost.com/publications/article/187086/marketing-lessons-from-team-obama.html#ixzz2KQani6dZ.
7 Alan R. Andreasen, *Social Marketing in the 21st Century* (Thousand Oaks, CA: Sage Publications, 2005).
8 Richard Robbins, "Marketing Lessons from Election '12'," *Huffington Post*, 13 November 2012.
9 Jon Fine, "Marketing Lessons from Obama's Campaign," *Bloomberg Businessweek*, 19 November 2008.
10 Ken Wheaton, "Lessons from the Obama Campaign Plus the Best Sarah Palin Moments of 2008," *Advertising Age*, 15 December 2008.

2 Lesson 1: Follow the Marketing Concept

1 C. Ziliani & S. Bellini, "Retail Micro-marketing Strategies and Competition," *The International Review of Retail, Distribution and Consumer Research, 14*(1) (2004): 7–18.
2 A.M. Brandenburger & B.J. Nalebuff, *Co-opetition* (London: Harper Collins, 1996), 8.
3 T. Jiang & A. Tuzhilin, "Dynamic Micro-targeting: Fitness-based Approach to Predicting Individual Preferences," *Knowledge and Information Systems, 19*(3) (2009): 337–60.
4 K.H. Jamieson, "Messages, Micro-targeting, and New Media Technologies," *The Forum, 11*(3) (October 2013): 429–35.
5 For a thorough discussion of this topic see: Bruce I. Newman, *The Marketing of the President: Political Marketing as Campaign Strategy* (Thousand Oaks, CA: Sage Publications, 1994); Wojciech Cwalina, Andrzej Falkowski, & Bruce I. Newman, *A Cross-Cultural Theory of Voter Behavior* (New York and London: The Haworth Press, Taylor & Francis Group, 2008); and Wojciech Cwalina, Andrzej Falkowski, & Bruce I. Newman, *Political Marketing: Theoretical and Strategic Foundations* (New York: M.E. Sharpe Publishing Company, 2011).
6 Newman, *The Marketing of the President.*
7 Ibid.
8 P.S.H. Leeflang, P.C. Verhoef, P. Dahlström, & T. Freundt, "Challenges and Solutions for Marketing in a Digital Era," *European Management Journal, 1* (February 2014):1–12.
9 For a discussion of the methodological, statistical, and strategic background behind the meetings that took place between myself and senior aides to President Clinton in 1995 and 1996, see: Bruce I. Newman, "A Predictive Model of Voter Behavior: The Repositioning of Bill Clinton," in Bruce I. Newman (Ed.), *Handbook of Political Marketing* (Thousand Oaks, CA: Sage Publications, 1999).
10 I. Rubenstein, "Voter Privacy in the Age of Big Data," *Wisconsin Law Review*, 26 April 2014.
11 Stewart J. Lawrence, "Ralph Reed: Return of the Church's Prodigal Son," *Time*, 6 June 2011: 16, 30.
12 Sasha Issenberg, "When It Comes to Targeting and Persuading Voters, the Obama Campaign Has a Massive, Insurmountable Advantage," *Huffington Post*, 29 October 2012.
13 Ibid.

14 P. Harris & A. Lock, "'Mind the Gap': The Rise of Political Marketing and a Perspective on Its Future Agenda," *European Journal of Marketing,* 44(3–4) (2010).

15 B. Schipper & H.Y. Woo, "Political Awareness and Microtargeting of Voters in Electoral Competition," Working Papers, University of California, Department of Economics, 12(4): 2012.

16 Newman, "A Predictive Model of Voter Behavior"; Bruce I. Newman & Jagdish N. Sheth, *A Theory of Political Choice Behavior* (New York: Praeger Press, 1987); Bruce I. Newman & Jagdish N. Sheth, "A Model of Primary Voter Behavior," *Journal of Consumer Research, 12* (1985): 178–87.

17 Dan Eggen, "Obama 2012: The Most Micro-targeted Campaign in History?" *Washington Post,* 15 January 2013. Available at: http://bigthink .com/age-of-engagement/obama-2012-the-most-micro-targeted-camapign-in-history.

18 Sasha Issenberg, "How Obama Used Big Data to Rally Voters," *MIT Technology Review,* 16 December 2012.

19 Richard Robbins, "Marketing Lessons from Election '12," *Huffington Post,* 13 November 2012.

20 Gil Press, "It's Your Data, Stupid," *Forbes,* 22 December 2012.

21 Ibid.

22 Nathan Abse, "Big Data Delivers on Campaign Promise: Microtargeted Political Advertising in Election," *iab, Innovations in Web Marketing and Advertising,* October 2012.

23 Ibid,

24 Ibid.

25 Lois Beckett, "Everything We Know (So Far) about Obama's Big Data Tactics," *ProPublica.Now,* 29 November 2012.

26 Gretchen Gavett, "Electing a President in a Microtargeted World," *Harvard Business Review,* 2 November 2012.

27 Robert Carraway, "Big Data, Small Bets," *Forbes,* 13 December 2012.

28 "Car Sellers Schooled in Disney Way of Loyal Customers," *Wall Street Journal,* 14 January 2013: B3.

29 Dan Berthiaume, "IBM Software Targets the 'Omni-Channel' Customer Experience," *CMS WIRE,* 15 January 2013.

30 "Making Ads More Interesting," *Google Official Blog,* 11 March 2009.

31 Charles Duhigg, "How Companies Learn Your Secrets," *New York Times,* 16 February 2012; Kashmir Hill, "How Target Figured Out a Teen Girl Was Pregnant before Her Father Did," *Forbes,* 16 February 2012.

32 Duhigg, "How Companies Learn Your Secrets"; Hill, "How Target Figured Out a Teen Girl Was Pregnant."

33 Nick Damoulakis, "10 Marketing Strategies for Non-Profit Organizations": accessed from http://blog.vistage.com, 15 February 2011.

34 "San Diego Internet Marketing and Web Development Firm Helps Local Non-Profit Charitable Housing Center with Upgraded Website," *Virtual-Strategy Magazine*, 28 December 2012.

35 "United Way Launches Social Media Campaign Aimed at Helping Inner City Population," *Target Market News: The Black Consumer Market Authority*, 15 October 2010.

36 R. Wilson, "A Public Relations Disaster; How Saving $1200 Cost United Airlines 10,772,839 Negative Views on YouTube," *Marketing Rocket Fuel* (2011). Available at: www.sentium.com.

37 Thomas B. Edsall, "Let the Nanotargeting Begin," *New York Times*, 15 April 2012.

38 For a discussion of this topic, see: Bruce Rogers, "Seeking CMOs: Must Know Big Data and Digital Marketing," *Forbes*, 15 January 2013; Carraway, "Big Data, Small Bets"; Paul Solman, "Breaking Down the Big Data," *Financial Times*, 15 January 2013.

39 For a discussion of this topic see: Rogers, "Seeking CMOs"; Carraway, "Big Data, Small Bets"; and Solman, "Breaking Down the Big Data."

3 Lesson 2: Use Technology Strategically

1 C. Cobb, "Same Game, New Rules: A Historic Presidential Campaign and What It Means for Our Digital Future," *Public Relations Tactics*, 15(12) (November 2008): 1–9. Available at: http://www.prsa.org/Intelligence/Tactics/Articles/view/7706/101/Same_game_new_rules_A_historic_presidential_campai.

2 *Wall Street Journal*, 26 October 2013: A4.

3 S. Cunningham, "Big Data, Marketing and Execution?" *Illinois Banker*, 99(1) (2014): 20.

4 P.S.H. Leeflang, P.C. Verhoef, P. Dahlström, & T. Freundt, "Challenges and Solutions for Marketing in a Digital Era," *European Management Journal*, 32(1) (February 2014): 1–12.

5 P. Russom, "Big Data Analytics," *TDWI Best Practices Report: Fourth Quarter* (2011). Available at: ftp://ftp.software.ibm.com/software/tw/Defining_Big_Data_through_3V_v.pdf.

6 D. Court, "Making Advanced Analytics Work for You," *Harvard Business Review* (October 2012): 78–83.

7 G. Marcus, "Steamrolled by Big Data," *The New Yorker*, 3 April 2013. Available at: http://www.newyorker.com/tech/elements/steamrolled-by-big-data.

8 J. Manyika, M. Chui, B. Brown, J. Bughin, R. Dobbs, C. Roxburgh, & A.H. Byers, "Big Data: The Next Frontier for Innovation, Competition, and Productivity,"*Insights & Publications* (McKinsey Global Institute, 2011). Available at: http://www.mckinsey.com/insights/business_technology/big_data_the_next_frontier_for_innovation.

9 For an overview of these issues, see: D. Boyd & K. Crawford, "Critical Questions for Big Data: Provocations for a Cultural, Technological, and Scholarly Phenomenon," *Information, Communication & Society, 15*(5) (2012): 662–79; G.C. Bowker, *Memory Practices in the Sciences* (Cambridge, MA: MIT Press, 2005); L. Burkholder (Ed.), *Philosophy and the Computer* (Boulder, CO, San Francisco, and Oxford: Westview Press, 1992); and M. Kranzberg, "Technology and History: Kranzberg's Laws," *Technology and Culture, 27*(3) (1986): 544–60.

10 Court, "Making Advanced Analytics Work for You."

11 Russom, "Big Data Analytics."

12 T. Harbert, "Big Data, Big Jobs?" *Computer World, 47*(1) (January 2013): 23–7.

13 K.K. Kambatla, "Trends in Big Data Analytics," *Journal of Parallel and Distributed Computing, 74*(7) (2014): 2561–73.

14 H. Chen, R.H.L. Chiang, & V.C. Story, "Business Intelligence and Analytics: From Big Data to Big Impact," *MIS Quarterly, 36*(4) (December 2012): 1165–88.

15 For a more in-depth discussion of customer analytics, see: T.H. Davenport, J.G. Harris, G.L. Jones, K.N. Lemon, & D. Norton, "The Dark Side of Customer Analytics," *Harvard Business Review, 85*(5) (May 2007): 37; J.L. Anderson, L.D. Jolly, & A.E. Fairhurst, "Customer Relationship Management in Retailing: A Content Analysis of Retail Trade Journals," *Journal of Retailing and Consumer Services, 14*(6) (2007): 394–9; P. Decker, "Data Mining's Hidden Dangers," *Banking Strategies, 74*(2) (1998): 6–14; M. Rogers, "Customer Strategy: Observations from the Trenches," *Journal of Marketing, 69*(4) (2005): 262–3; T.H. Bijmolt, P.S. Leeflang, F. Block, M. Eisenbeiss, B.G. Hardie, A. Lemmens, & P. Saffert, "Analytics for Customer Engagement," *Journal of Service Research, 13*(3) (2010): 341–56; R. Deshpande, "Paradigms Lost: On Theory and Method in Research in Marketing," *Journal of Marketing, 47*(4) (1983):101–10; J. Van Doorn, K. Lemon, V. Mittal, S. Nass, D. Pick, P. Pimer, & P. Verhoef, "Customer Engagement Behavior: Theoretical Foundations and Research Directions," *Journal of Service Research, 13*(3) (2010): 253–66; P.C. Verhoef, J. Van Doorn, & M. Dorotic, "Customer Value Management: An Overview and Research Agenda," *Marketing-Journal of Research and Management, 3*(2)

(2007): 105–20; F.V.Wangenheim, & T. Bayon, "The Chain from Customer Satisfaction via Word-of-Mouth Referrals to New Customer Acquisition," *Journal of the Academy of Marketing Science*, 35(2) (2007): 233–49.

16 Leslie Wayne, "Democrats Take Page from Their Rival's Playbook," *New York Times*, 1 November 2008: A15.

17 S. Towns, "A Vote for Big Data," *Government Technology*, 25(12) (2012): 6.

18 Engage Research, *Inside the Cave* (London, 2014). Available at: http://enga.ge/projects/inside-the-cave/ http://engagedc.com/download/Inside%20the%20Cave.pdf.

19 G. Shen, "Big Data, Analytics and Elections," *Analytics* (January/February 2013): 40–4.

20 J. Sides, "Data and Analytics Have Changed Campaigns. Now What's Next?" *Washington Post*, 23 January 2014. Available at: http://www.washingtonpost.com/blogs/monkey-cage/wp/2014/01/23/data-and-analytics-have-changed-campaigns-now-whats-next/.

21 Molly Ball, "Obama's Edge: The Ground Game That Could Put Him over the Top," *Atlantic*, 24 October 2012. Available at: http://www.theatlantic.com/politics/archive/2012/10/obamas-edge-the-ground-game-that-could-put-him-over-the-top/264031/.

22 Lois Beckett, "Everything We Know (So Far) about Obama's Big Data Tactics," *ProPublica.Now*, 29 November 2012. Available at: http://www.propublica.org/article/everything-we-know-so-far-about-obamas-big-data-operation.

23 Ibid.

24 Ibid.

25 Jennifer Rooney, "For CMOs, Agility Is the New Black: Survey," *Forbes*, 28 January 2013: 11. Available at: http://www.forbes.com/sites/jenniferrooney/2013/01/28/for-cmos-agility-is-the-new-black-survey.

26 *Fortune*, 18 November 2013: 49.

27 *Wall Street Journal*, 8 November 2013: B1–B2.

28 Ibid.

29 *Wall Street Journal*, 14 November 2012: B7.

30 Marisa Peacock, "Text Analytics: What Are They, Why Are They Important to CXM?" *CMS WiRE*, 10 January 2013. Available at: http://www.cmswire.com/cms/customer-experience/text-analytics-what-are-they-why-are-they-important-to-cxm-019073.php.

31 Colin Wood, "6 Ways to Optimize Gov-to-Citizen Communication," *Government Technology*, 25 January 2013. Available at: http://www.govtech.com/education/6-Ways-to-Optimize-Gov-to-Citizen-Communication.html.

32 Esra Klein, "How the iPod President Crashed: Obama's Broken Technology Promise," *Bloomberg BusinessWeek*, 31 October 2013: 14–17. Available at: http://www.bloomberg.com/bw/articles/2013-10-31/obamas-broken-promise-of-better-government-through-technology.

33 David Milton Brent, "New Report Blasts Super PACs as 'Bad for Democracy,'" *Progress Illinois*, 13 February 2012. Available at: http://progressillinois.com/posts/content/2012/02/13/new-report-blasts-super-pacs-bad-democracy.

34 Klein, "How the iPod President Crashed."

4 Lesson 3: Integrate Research Methods

1 James Mahoney & Gary Goertz, "A Tale of Two Cultures: Contrasting Quantitative and Qualitative Research," *Political Analysis*, 14(2006): 227–49.

2 Wojciech Cwalina, Andrzej Falkowski, & Bruce I. Newman, *A Cross-Cultural Theory of Voter Behavior* (New York and London: The Haworth Press, Taylor & Francis Group, 2008).

3 For a discussion of these methods see: P. Lazarsfeld, B. Berelson, & H. Gaudet, *The People's Choice: How the Voter Makes up His Mind in a Presidential Campaign* (New York: Columbia University Press, 1944).

4 M.P. Wattenberg, *The Rise of Candidate-Centered Politics: Presidential Elections of the 1980s* (Cambridge, MA: Harvard University Press, 1995).

5 S.H. Chaffee & R.N. Rimal, "Time of Vote Decision and Openness to Persuasion," in D. Mutz, P. Sniderman, & R. Brody (Eds.), *Political Persuasion and Attitude Change* (Ann Arbor: University of Michigan Press, 1996).

6 T.M. Holbrook, *Do Campaigns Matter?* (Thousand Oaks, CA: Sage Publications, 1996).

7 Robert G. Kaiser, "Hearts, Not Minds," *Washington Post*, 30 June 2008.

8 Ibid.

9 Michael Oreskes, "Lee Atwater, Master of Tactics for Bush and G.O.P., Dies at 40," *New York Times*, 30 March 1991. Available at: http://www.nytimes.com/1991/03/30/obituaries/lee-atwater-master-of-tactics-for-bush-and-gop-dies-at-40.html?pagewanted=2.

10 Kaiser, "Hearts, Not Minds."

11 Paul Hyman, "'Small Data' Enabled Prediction of Obama's Win, Say Economists," *Communications of the ACM*, 56(5) (May 2013): 23–5.

12 Note: For an overview of polling in politics, see: R. Curtin, S. Presser, & E. Singer, "Changes in Telephone Survey Nonresponse over the Past Quarter Century," *Public Opinion Quarterly*, 69(87) (2005): 98; T. Rosenstiel, "Political Polling and the New Media Culture: A Case of More Being

Less," *Public Opinion Quarterly*, 69(5) (2005): 698–715; J.S. Fishkin, *Democracy and Deliberation: New Directions for Democratic Reform* (New Haven, CT: Yale University Press, 1991); J.S. Fishkin & R.C. Luskin, "Experimenting with a Democratic Ideal: Deliberative Polling and Public Opinion," *Acta Politica*, 40(3) (2005): 284–98.

13 Hyman, " 'Small Data' Enabled Prediction of Obama's Win."

14 Mahoney & Goertz, "A Tale of Two Cultures."

15 Kaiser, "Hearts, Not Minds."

16 Ed Pilkington & Amanda Michel, "Conservative Super PACs Turn to Social Media and Internet to Expand Reach," *The Guardian*, 29 June 2012. Available at: http://www.theguardian.com/world/2012/jun/29/conservative-super-pacs-social-media.

17 "How to Increase Leads with Social Media," *The Telegraph Blog*, 5 February 2013. Available at: http://www.nashuatelegraph.com/digitalmarketing/digitalmarketingblog/992649-459/how-to-increase-leads-with-social-media.html.

18 Anne Creedon, "Three Key Takeaways from Nielsen's 2012 Social Media Report," *Nielsen's 2012 Social Media Report*, 5 February 2013. Available at: http://nonprofitquarterly.org/2013/02/05/three-key-takeaways-from-nielsens-2012-social-media-report/.

19 Ibid.

20 Connie Sung Moyle, "Non-Profits Investing More Time, Money in Social Media," *Non-Profit Marketing*, 6 December 2012. Available at: http://www.verticalresponse.com/blog/non-profits-investing-more-time-money-social-media/.

21 Alex Kantrowitz, "Next Pope Will Inherit an Established Social Media Presence with Room to Grow," *Forbes*, 11 February 2013. Available at: http://www.forbes.com/sites/alexkantrowitz/2013/02/11/next-pope-will-inherit-an-established-social-media-presence-with-room-to-grow/.

22 Suresh Naidu & Dolrian T. Warren, "What Labor Can Learn from the Obama Campaign," *The Nation*, 13 February 2013. Available at: http://www.thenation.com/article/what-labor-can-learn-obama-campaign/.

23 Ibid.

24 K. Sandberg, "Marketing Feature – Focusing on the Benefits – Sharpening the Focus of Focus Groups," *Harvard Business School*, 8 July 2002. Available at: http://hbswk.hbs.edu/archive/3004.html.

25 For a discussion of this topic see: Creedon, "Three Key Takeaways from Nielsen's 2012 Social Media Report"; and Bill Smith, "City Offers Non-profits Social Media 'Boot Camp,'" *Social Media Boot Camp*, 6 February 2013. Available at: http://evanstonnow.com/story/education/

bill-smith/2013-02-06/54594/city-offers-non-profits-social-media-boot-camp.
26 Ibid.
27 Ibid.

5 Lesson 4: Develop a Unique Brand Identity

1 Itamar Simonson & Emanuel Rosen, "Three Long-Held Concepts Every Marketer Should Rethink," 22 January 2014. Available at: http://blogs.hbr.org/2014/01/three-long-held-concepts-every-marketer-should-rethink/.
2 For a more in-depth discussion from some of the classic articles in this area, see: K.L. Keller, "Building Customer-Based Brand Equity: A Blueprint for Creating Strong Brands," *Marketing Management, 10* (July/August 2001): 15–19; K.L. Keller, B. Sternthal, & A. Tybout, "Three Questions You Need to Ask about Your Brand," *Harvard Business Review, 80*(9) (September 2002): 80–9; K.L Keller & D.R. Lehmann, "Brands and Branding: Research Findings and Future Priorities," *Marketing Science, 25*(6) (2006): 740–59; P. Kotler & K.L. Keller, *Marketing Management,* 12th ed. (Upper Saddle River, NJ: Prentice-Hall, 2006). See also the following classic references on branding: D.D. Aaker & R. Jacobson, "The Financial Information Content of Perceived Quality," *Journal of Marketing Research, 31* (May 1994): 191–201; K.L. Keller, *Strategic Brand Management: Building, Measuring, and Managing Brand Equity,* 2nd ed. (Paramus, NJ: Prentice Hall 2002); V.R. Rao, M.K. Agarwal, & D. Dahlhoff, "How Is Manifest Branding Strategy Related to the Intangible Value of a Corporation?" *Journal of Marketing, 68*(4) (2004): 126–41.
3 For a discussion of emotional branding, see: D. Atkin, *The Culting of Brands: Turn Your Customers into True Believers* (New York: Penguin, 2005); B. Cova & V. Cova, "The Tribalization of Society and Its Impact on the Conduct of Marketing," *European Journal of Marketing, 36*(5–6) (2002): 595–620; M. Gobé, *Emotional Branding: The New Paradigm for Connecting Brands to People* (New York: Allworth Press, 2001); S. Fournier, "Consumers and Their Brands: Developing Relationship Theory in Consumer Research," *Journal of Consumer Research, 24* (March 1998): 343–74; A.M. Muniz, Jr., & T.C. O'Guinn, "Brand Community," *Journal of Consumer Research, 27*(4) (2001): 412–32; T.C. O'Guinn & A.M. Muniz, Jr., "Communal Consumption and the Brand," chapter 13 in S. Ratneshwar & D.G. Mick, *Inside Consumption: Consumer Motives, Goals, and Desires* (Abingdon: Routledge, 2005); K. Roberts, *Lovemarks: The Future beyond Brands* (New York: Powerhouse Books, 2004); C.J. Thompson, A. Rindfleisch, & Z.Arsel,

"Emotional Branding and the Strategic Value of the Doppelgänger Brand Image," *Journal of Marketing*, 70(1) (2006): 50–6.

4 Margaret Scammel, *Consumer Democracy* (Cambridge: Cambridge University Press, 2014).

5 Ron Romanik, "Obama the Brand 2012: Behind the Curve," *Beneath the Brand: Covering the Changing World of Branding* (2012). Available at: http://www.talentzoo.com/beneath-the-brand/blog_news.php?articleID=14452.

6 A. Goneos-Malka, A. Grobler, & A. Strashheim, "Suggesting New Communication Tactics Using Digital Media to Optimize Postmodern Traits in Marketing," *Communicatio*, 39(1) (2013): 122–43.

7 A. Chintakananda & D.P. McIntyre, "Market Entry in the Presence of Network Effects: A Real Options Perspective," *Journal of Management*, 40(6) (September 2014): 1535–57.

8 S. Polit, "The Organizational Impacts of Managing Social Marketing Interventions," *Social Marketing Quarterly*, 18(2012): 124. Retrieved from: http://smq.sagepub.com/content/18/2/124.

9 D. Fazekas, "Strategy Trumps Tactics," *Smart Business Philadelphia*, 7(5) (January 2013): 7.

10 L. Manternach, "First Strategy, Then Tactics," *Corridor Business Journal*, 10(46) (2014): 13.

11 B. Nguyen, M. Li, & C.H. Chen, "The Targeted and Nontargeted Framework: Differential Impact of Marketing Tactics on Customer Perceptions," *Journal of Targeting, Measurement and Analysis for Marketing*, 20 (May 2012): 96–108.

12 Margaret Talev, "Obama Threads Digs at Romney into Campaign Rhetoric," *Bloomberg Business*, 17 August 2012.

13 Romanik, "Obama the Brand 2012: Behind the Curve."

14 Ibid.

15 See chapter 2 for a more in-depth discussion of my role in the Clinton White House.

16 Donovan Slack, "Obama: A Brand in Search of a Slogan," *Politico*, 7 April 2012: 1.

17 Alexis C. Madrigal, "When the Nerds Go Marching In," *The Atlantic*, 17 November 2012. Available at: www.theatlantic.com/technology/print/2012.

18 Romanik, "Obama the Brand 2012: Behind the Curve."

19 For a thorough discussion of the role of consultants in political campaigns, see: Dennis Johnson, *The Routledge Handbook of Political Management* (New York: Routledge, 2008); Dennis Johnson, *No Place for Amateurs: How Political Consultants Are Reshaping American Democracy* (New York: Routledge, 2001);

and James A. Thurber & Candice J. Nelson (Eds.), *Campaign Warriors: Political Consultants in Elections* (Washington, DC: Brookings Institution, 2000).

20 Bruce I. Newman, *The Mass Marketing of Politics: Democracy in an Age of Manufactured Images* (Thousand Oaks, CA: Sage Publications, 1999).

21 Simonson & Rosen, "Three Long-Held Concepts Every Marketer Should Rethink."

22 Linda Killian, "Five Myths about Independent Voters," 17 May 2012. Available at: http://www.washingtonpost.com/opinions/five-myths-about-independent-voters/2012/05/17/gIQAZmGyWU_story.html.

23 Simonson & Rosen, "Three Long-Held Concepts Every Marketer Should Rethink."

24 N. Kylander & C. Stone, "The Role of Brand in the Nonprofit Sector," *Stanford Social Innovation Review* (Spring 2012). Available at: http://www.ssireview.org/articles/entry/the_role_of_brand_in_the_nonprofit_sector.

25 Barry Cooke, "5 Social Media Publishing Lessons Brands Learned This Year," *Content Marketing Institute*, 26 November 2012. Available at: http://contentmarketinginstitute.com/2012/11/social-media-publishing-lessons-brands-learned/.

26 Jeff Elder, "Social Media Fail to Live Up to Early Marketing Hype," *Wall Street Journal*, 23 June 2014: B1–B2.

27 Mark Johanson, "Discover America: US Invites Tourists with First-Ever Unified Campaign from Brand USA," 7 November 2011. Available at: www.ibtimes.com.

28 Mike Girard, "5 Social Media Fundraising Tips for Non-Profits, Strategy," inShare.com, 22 June 2012. Available at: http://www.salesforcemarketing-cloud.com/blog/category/social-media/strategy/page/29/.

29 Ibid.

30 Julie Cottineau, "Six Success Strategies for Building a Stronger Brand," *Journal of Brand Strategy*, 1(3) (Autumn 2012): 240–6.

31 Ginger Gibson, "Jim Messina: What I Learned in the Election," *Politico*, 20 November 2012. Available at: http://www.politico.com/news/stories/1112/84103.html.

32 Ed Pilkington & Amanda Michel, "Conservative Super PACs Turn to Social Media and Internet to Expand Reach," *The Guardian*, 29 June 2012. Available at: http://www.theguardian.com/world/2012/jun/29/conservative-super-pacs-social-media.

33 G. Llopis, "6 Brand Strategies Most CMOs Fail to Execute," *Forbes*, 10 March 2014. Available at: http://www.forbes.com/sites/glennllopis/2014/03/10/6-brand-strategies-that-most-cmos-fail-to-execute/.

34 Ibid.

6 Lesson 5: Create a Winning Advertising Strategy

1 Ken Wheaton, "Lessons from the Obama Campaign," *Advertising Age*, 15 December 2008.

2 For a review of the role of advertising and persuasion in both the commercial and the social marketplaces, see Wojciech Cwalina, Andrzej Falkowski, & Bruce I. Newman, "Persuasion in the Political Context: Opportunities and Threats," chapter 4 in David W. Stewart (Ed.), *The Handbook of Persuasion and Social Marketing* (New York: Routledge, 2014), 61–128.

3 For a thorough review of the role of advertising from a political communication perspective, and the impact on recent political campaigns, see Richard M. Perloff, *The Dynamics of Persuasion: Communication and Attitudes in the 21st Century* (New York: Routledge, 2013).

4 For some classic books and articles on this subject see: D.A. Aaker & A. Biel (Eds.), *Brand Equity and Advertising: Advertising's Role in Building Strong Brands* (New York: Psychology Press, 2013); B. Edelman, M. Ostrovsky, & M. Schwarz, "Internet Advertising and the Generalized Second Price Auction: Selling Billions of Dollars Worth of Keywords," National Bureau of Economic Research Working Paper No. 11765 (November 2005), also published in *American Economic Review*, 97(1) (March 2007): 242–59; S. Ewen, *Captains of Consciousness: Advertising and the Social Roots of the Consumer Culture* (New York: Basic Books, 2008); M.M. Tsang, S.C. Ho, & T.P. Liang, "Consumer Attitudes toward Mobile Advertising: An Empirical Study," *International Journal of Electronic Commerce*, 8(3) (2004): 65–78; F.D. Davis, "Perceived Usefulness, Perceived Ease of Use, and User Acceptance of Information Technology," *Management Information Systems Quarterly*, 13(3) (1989): 319–40; F.D. Davis, R.P. Bagozzi, & P.R. Warshaw, "User Acceptance of Computer Technology: A Comparison of Two Theoretical Models," *Management Science*, 35(8) (1989): 982–1003.

5 D. Kreiss, "Acting in the Public Sphere: The 2008 Obama Campaign's Strategic Use of New Media to Shape Narratives of the Presidential Race," *Media, Movements, and Political Change Research in Social Movements, Conflicts and Change*, 33 (2012): 195–223.

6 Ibid.

7 C. Vargo, L. Guo, M. McCombs, & D. Shaw, "Network Issue Agendas on Twitter during the 2012 U.S. Presidential Election," *Journal of Communication*, 64(2) (2014): 296–316.

8 Amy Gershkoff, "Obama's Media Adviser Tells Us the 5 Most Important Ad Tactics from the Presidential Campaign," *Business Insider*, 12 November 2012. Available at:www.businessinsider.com.

9   "2012 Presidential Campaign Finance Explorer," *Washington Post Graphic,* 7 December 2012.

10 Elizabeth Wilner, "Romney and Republicans Outspent Obama, but Couldn't Out-Advertise Him," *Advertising Age,* 9 November 2012. Available at: http://adage.com/article/campaign-trail/romney-outspent-obama-advertise/238241/.

11 Jim Rutenberg & Jeremy W. Peters, "Obama Outspending Romney on TV Ads," *New York Times,* 3 October 2012.

12 "2012 Presidential Campaign Finance Explorer."

13 "Obama Campaign Media Strategy Focuses on Non-Traditional Outlets," *Huffington Post Blog,* 18 September 2012.

14 Jim Kuhnhenn & Nancy Benac, "2012 Presidential Election: Obama, Mitt Romney Sprint toward Finish Line," *Huffington Post,* 3 November 2012.

15 Gershkoff, "Obama's Media Adviser Tells Us the 5 Most Important Ad Tactics."

16 Richard Parker, "Social and Anti-Social Media," *New York Times,* 15 November 2012. Available at: http://campaignstops.blogs.nytimes.com/2012/11/15/social-and-anti-social-media/?_r=0.

17 Sarah Algethami, "Digital Ad Space Is Growing Nicely and Fetching Profits," *Gulf News,* 13 February 2013.

18 Amy Chozick & Michael J. De La Merced, "Time Warner Considers Spinning Off Some of Its Magazines," *New York Times,* 13 February 2013.

19 "Advertising, Video and Wearable Tech – the Biggest Emerging Mobile Trends for 2014," *The Star,* 21 February 2014. Available at: *TheStar.com.*

20 Ibid.

21 Ibid.

22 E. Walter, "2014 Digital Trends and Predictions from Marketing Thought Leaders," *Forbes,* 7 December 2013.

23 Chunka Mui, "These 6 Technologies Will Make or Break Every Information-Intensive Company – Including Yours," *Forbes,* 2 February 2014. Available at: http://www.forbes.com/sites/chunkamui/2014/02/20/these-6-technologies-will-make-or-break-every-information-intensive-company-including-yours/.

7 Lesson 6: Build a Relationship with Your Customers

1   A.M. Kaplan & M. Haenlein, "Users of the World, Unite! The Challenges and Opportunities of Social Media," *Business Horizons,* 53(1) (2010): 59–68.

2   W.G. Mangold & D.J. Faulds, "Social Media: The New Hybrid Element of the Promotion Mix," *Business Horizons,* 52(4) (2009): 357–65. For a more

in-depth discussion of the application of research findings in the field of communication, see W. Schramm & D.F. Roberts, *The Process and Effects of Mass Communication* (Urbana: University of Illinois Press, 1971).

3 For classic works in this area, see: R.W. Palmatier, R.P. Dant, D. Grewal, & K.R. Evans, "Factors Influencing the Effectiveness of Relationship Marketing: A Meta-analysis," *Journal of Marketing, 70*(4) (2006): 136–53; R.Srinivasan & C. Moorman, "Strategic Firm Commitments and Rewards for Customer Relationship Management in Online Retailing," *Journal of Marketing, 69* (2005): 193–200; L.L Berry, "Relationship Marketing," in L.L. Berry, G.L. Shostack, & G.D Upah (Eds.), *Emerging Perspectives on Services Marketing*, Proceedings Series, American Marketing Association (Chicago: American Marketing Association,1983); C. Grönroos, "The Relationship Marketing Process: Communication, Interaction, Dialogue, Value," *Journal of Business & Industrial Marketing, 19*(2) (2004): 99–113; B.B. Jackson,"Build Customer Relationships That Last," *Harvard Business Review, 63* (1985): 120–8; E. Gummesson, "Return on Relationships (ROR): The Value of Relationship Marketing and CRM in Business-to-Business Contexts," *Journal of Business & Industrial Marketing, 19*(2) (2004): 136–48; M. Ahearne, C.B. Bhattacharya, & T. Gruen, "Antecedents and Consequences of Customer-Company Identification: Expanding the Role of Relationship Marketing," *Journal of Applied Psychology, 90*(3) (2005): 574.

4 Dennis Michalis, "The Key to Building Customer Relationships: Serve Your Own Team First," *Forbes*, 15 November 2012. Available at: http://www.forbes.com/sites/microsoftdynamics/2012/11/15/creating-new-relationships/.

5 J. DiGrazia, K. McKelvey, J. Bollen, & F. Rojas, "More Tweets, More Votes: Social Media as a Quantitative Indicator of Political Behavior," *PLOS One*, 27 November 2013.

6 J. Bronstein, "Like Me! Analyzing the 2012 U.S. Presidential Candidates' Facebook Pages," *Online Information Review, 37*(2) (2013): 173–82.

7 T. Towner, "All Political Participation," *Social Science Computer Review, 31* (2013): 527.

8 T. Goodnow, "Facing Off: A Comparative Analysis of Obama and Romney Facebook Timeline Photographs," *American Behavioral Scientist, 57*(11) (2013): 1584–95; originally published online 24 May 2013.

9 Richard Parker, "Social and Anti-Social Media," *New York Times*, 15 November 2012.

10 K. Smith & E. Bratt, "The Obama Playbook: How Digital Marketing and Social Media Won the Election," *MarketingProfs*, Special Report, 2009, marketingprofs LLC. Available at: http://cdn2.hubspot.net/hub/93656/file-1912674360-pdf/docs/obamaplaybook_vc.pdf.

11 Daniel Nations, "How Barack Obama Is Using Web 2.0 to Run for President." Available at: http://webtrends.about.com/od/web20/a/obama-web.htm.

12 Michael Scherer, "Inside the Secret World of the Data Crunchers Who Helped Obama Win," 7 November 2012. Available at: http://swampland.time.com/2012/11/07/inside-the-secret-world-of-quants-and-data-crunchers-who-helped-obama-win/.

13 Julianna Goldman, "Obama Winning Social Media, if #Hashtagwars Really Matter," *Bloomberg Business*, 22 October 2012.

14 Jenna Wortham, "Campaigns Use Social Media to Lure Younger Voters," *New York Times*, 7 October 2012.

15 "Barack Obama and the Facebook Election," *US News and World Report*, 19 November 2008.

16 Pew Research Center, Journalism and Media Staff, "How the Presidential Candidates Use the Web and Social Media," *Pew Research Center, Journalism & Media*, 15 August 2012. Available at: http://www.journalism.org/2012/08/15/how-presidential-candidates-use-web-and-social-media/.

17 Jose Antonio Vargas,"'Obama Raised Half a Billion Online," *Washington Post*, 20 November 2008. Available at: http://voices.washingtonpost.com/44/2008/11/20/obama_raised_half_a_billion_on.html.

18 Scherer, "Inside the Secret World of the Data Crunchers Who Helped Obama Win."

19 Tim Mullaney, "Social Media Is Reinventing How Business Is Done," *USA Today*, 16 May 2012. Available at: http://usatoday30.usatoday.com/money/economy/story/2012-05-14/social-media-economy-companies/55029088/1.

20 Shel Israel, "Will Marketing Muck Up Social Media?" *Forbes*, 5 July 2012.

21 Brad Stone, "Clicking for a Cause," *New York Times*, 12 November 2009.

22 Israel, "Will Marketing Muck Up Social Media?"

23 Beth Kanter, "4 Ways Social Media Is Changing the Non-profit World," *Mashable*, 22 May 2009. Available at: http://mashable.com/2009/05/22/non-profit-social-media/.

24 Blog, "How Obama Won with Social Media," *The Dragonfly Effect*, n.d. Available at: http://www.dragonflyeffect.com/blog/dragonfly-in-action/case-studies/the-obama-campaign/.

25 Ahrif Sarumi, "How Nonprofit Leaders Avoid Social Media Burnout," 21 January 2013. Available at: www.blogworld.com.

26 David Mielach, "5 Social Media Biz Strategies You'll See This Year," *Business News Daily*, 3 January 2013. Available at: http://www.businessnewsdaily.com/3669-social-media-strategies.html.

27 C. Shih, "What's the Endgame for Social Media?" *Harvard Business Review*, 9 January 2014.

8 Lesson 7: Be Prepared to Engage in Crisis Management

1 M. Eid & J. Bresolin Slade, "A Triad of Crisis Communication in the United States: Social Networks for Social Change in the Obama Era," *International Journal of Technoethics*, 3(4) (2012): 1–21. Retrieved from Sage.com.
2 A. Kampf & N. Löwenheim, "Rituals of Apology in the Global Arena," *Security Dialogue*, 43(1) (February 2012): 43–60.Retrieved from Sage.com.
3 For a review of definitions and theory in crisis management, see: B. Faulkner, "Towards a Framework for Tourism Disaster Management," *Tourism Management*, 22(2) (2001): 135–47; T. Pauchant & I. Mitroff, *Transforming the Crisis-Prone Organization: Preventing Individual, Organizational, and Environmental Tragedies* (San Francisco: Jossey-Bass, 1992); B. Richardson, "Crisis Management and Management Strategy – Time to 'Loop the Loop?'" *Disaster Prevention and Management*, 3(3) (1994): 59–80; B.W. Ritchie, "Chaos, Crises and Disasters: A Strategic Approach to Crisis Management in the Tourism Industry," *Tourism Management*, 25(6) (2004): 669–83. For a review of more classic works in this area, see: K.D. Sweetser & E. Metzgar, "Communicating during Crisis: Use of Blogs as a Relationship Management Tool," *Public Relations Review*, 33(3) (2007): 340-2; A. Boin, P.'t Hart, E. Stern, & B. Sundelius, *The Politics of Crisis Management. Public Leadership under Pressure* (New York: Cambridge University Press, 2005); R. Axelrod & M.D. Cohen, *Harnessing Complexity: Organizational Implications of a Scientific Frontier* (New York: Free Press, 1999); L.K. Comfort, "Self-Organization in Complex Systems," *Journal of Public Administration Research and Theory*, 4(3) (1994): 393–410; L.K. Comfort, "Crisis Management in Hindsight: Cognition, Communication, Coordination, and Control," *Public Administration Review*, 67(s1) (2007): 189–197; D.F. Kettl, *System under Stress: Homeland Security and American Politics.*, 2nd ed. (Washington, DC: CQ Press, 2006); D. Kiel, *Managing Chaos and Complexity in Government* (San Francisco: Jossey-Bass, 1994).; G.A. Klein, J. Orasanu, & R. Calderwood, (Eds.), *Decision Making in Action: Models and Methods* (Norwood, NJ: Ablex, 1993); A. Boin, & A. McConnell, "Preparing for Critical Infrastructure Breakdowns: The Limits of Crisis Management and the Need for Resilience," *Journal of Contingencies and Crisis Management*, 15(1) (2007),: 50–9; C. Perrow, *Normal Accidents: Living with High-Risk Technologies*, 2nd ed., (Princeton, NJ: Princeton University Press, 1999); B.A. Turner, *Man-Made Disasters* (London: Wykeham, 1978).

4 T. Brochers & J.L. Miller, "Bain and Political Capital in the 2012 GOP Primary Debates," *American Behavioral Scientist, 58*(4) (April 2014): 574–90. Retrieved from Sage.com.

5 Aviva Shen, "Karl Rove: Obama Was 'Lucky' That Hurricane Sandy Hit," thinkprogress.org, 8 November 2012.

6 Mortimer Zuckerman, "Obama and the 'Competency Crisis,'" *Wall Street Journal*, 25 August 2011.

7 "Hurricane Katrina Statistics Fast Facts," CNN Library, 23 August 2013: 2. Available at: cnn.com.

8 Ibid.

9 S. Alfano, "Race an Issue in Katrina Response," cbsnews.com, 3 September 2005.

10 Kelli Dugan, "Carnival Triumph: A Case Study in Crisis Management," www.blog.al.com, 16 February 2013.

11 Alfano, "Race an Issue in Katrina Response."

12 Ibid.

13 J. Rainey, "Hurricane Sandy Is a Crisis and Opportunity for Obama, Romney," latimes.com, 29 October 2012.

14 Shen, "Karl Rove: Obama Was 'Lucky' That Hurricane Sandy Hit."

15 Rainey, "Hurricane Sandy Is a Crisis and Opportunity for Obama, Romney"; K. Walsh, "A Tale of Two Storms: Comparing Bush and Obama's Hurricane Response," *US News*, 31 October 2012.

16 Dugan, 'Carnival Triumph."

17 "Carnival Cruise Tells Passengers They Can Keep the Bathrobes in Total PR Fiasco," *Huffington Post* blog, 14 February 2013.

18 John M. Holcomb, "Let's Give BP Some Credit," *Forbes*, 6 August 2010.

19 Ibid.

20 C.V. Harquail, "10 Reasons Why the Komen Foundation Should Stop Lying about Its Motives," *Forbes*, 8 February 2012.

21 blog, "What Not to Do in a Crisis," 3 February 2012.

22 Paul Leinwand & Cesare Mainardi, "The Cure for the Not-for-Profit Crisis," *Harvard Business Review* blog, 11 October 2011.

23 John R. Kimberly, "How BP Blew Crisis Management 101," CNN.com, 21 June 2010.

24 "Best Research Practices for Crisis Management," Ipsos.com (n.d.).

25 Ibid.

26 Tara Weiss, "The Art of Crisis Management," *Forbes*, 10 August 2006.

27 Peter Apps, "Crisis Management Puts Huge Strains on Firms, CEOs," Reuters, 30 March 2011.

28 Kimberly, "How BP Blew Crisis Management 101."

29 Stephanie Chen, "Crisis Management 101: What Can BP CEO Hayward's Mistakes Teach Us?" www.cnn.com, 27 July 2010.
30 Davia Temin, "Crisis Management 1001: Reputation Rehab," *Forbes*, 12 August 2010.

9 Concluding Remarks

1 Bruce I. Newman, *The Marketing of the President: Political Marketing as Campaign Strategy* (Thousand Oaks, CA: Sage Publications, 1994).
2 Bruce I. Newman, *Handbook of Political Marketing* (Thousand Oaks, CA: Sage Publications, 1999).
3 Christine B. Williams & Bruce I. Newman, *Political Marketing in Retrospective and Prospective* (New York: Routledge, 2013).
4 Mortimer Zuckerman, "The Full-Time Scandal of Part-Time America," *Wall Street Journal*, 14 July, 2014: A15.
5 Reid J. Epstein, "Pollsters Missed Their Mark in Many States," *Wall Street Journal*, 7 November 2014: A5.
6 For a discussion of the latest technological advances in marketing used in political campaigns, see: Bruce I. Newman, Editor-in-Chief, *Journal of Political Marketing* (Philadelphia: Taylor & Francis Publishing Co.).

Index